SEE WHAT I MEAN

HOW TO USE COMICS TO COMMUNICATE IDEAS

Kevin Cheng

Rosenfeld Media
Brooklyn, New York

See What I Mean: How to Use Comics to Communicate Ideas
By Kevin Cheng

Rosenfeld Media, LLC

457 Third Street, #4R

Brooklyn, New York

11215 USA

On the Web: www.rosenfeldmedia.com

Please send errors to: errata@rosenfeldmedia.com

Publisher: Louis Rosenfeld

Managing Editor: Marta Justak

Interior Layout Tech: Danielle Foster

Cover Design: The Heads of State

Indexer: Nancy Guenther

Proofreader: Sue Boshers

ISBN: 1-933820-27-6

ISBN-13: 978-1-933820-27-9

LCCN: 2012950615

Printed and bound in the United States of America

DEDICATION

To Coley, who always sees what I mean. And to Mum and Dad, who never told me to stop drawing silly cartoons.

HOW TO USE THIS BOOK

As this is a book about using comics to communicate ideas, you might expect that the book itself would be in comic form, much like Scott McCloud's *Understanding Comics*. That's partially what I did with this book, but everyone learns and digests information differently so I decided to actually provide two different ways to read the book. With the exception of the first and last chapters, which are both full comics, each chapter has two versions. The beginning of each chapter has a short comic that summarizes the material in that chapter, followed by much more in-depth writing on the topic. You'll also find that the art in the summaries is deliberately quite rough to illustrate just how little you need to draw to get ideas across.

Which version you choose to read is completely up to you. You might read only the comics, all the comics' summaries first followed by the text, or everything in page order. Regardless, I think you will get something from it.

While there are many books exploring how to make comics for aspiring professionals and other books exploring the science and inner workings of comics, this book differs because it's focused on applying comics for practical uses. It's a mix of "How do I do it?" "Why should I use this?" and "When should I use it?"

You'll learn why comics are a powerful medium. Then you'll learn how to create comics through step-by-step examples. And finally, you'll discover the different ways to apply comics and how to convince others to try using them. Throughout the book, I've included examples and case studies from other experts in design, comics, animation, and more.

Who Should Read This Book?

This book is written for anyone involved in dreaming up ideas and making those ideas a reality. If you're a leader in your team or company, comics can help you convey your high-level vision to the team. If you're a designer or engineer, comics can help you understand your product better and speed up development. For marketers, you'll see how comics can be used to teach your customers about your product. You don't need to be the one making the comics to get value from this book, but you might be surprised how easy it is to create them yourself.

What's in This Book?

This book is organized into three main sections.

- **Why Comics?** The first couple of chapters explore what comics are and why they're a powerful medium. Understanding the medium's strengths can help you decide when it's appropriate to use it.

- **Making a Comic.** The next five chapters go through how to create comics. We'll carry one example through from beginning to end over the course of the chapters—starting with basic drawing techniques, followed by defining and writing the story, and ending with some tips on how to lay out and polish the comic.

- **Using Comics.** The final chapters explore some other applications for comics including marketing, user research, and conveying vision. There's also a chapter specifically dedicated to how you can convince other people to try out comics.

What Comes with This Book?

This book's companion website (🐘 rosenfeldmedia.com/books/comics) contains links to a number of resources such as articles, templates, software, research, and tools. I've also provided some templates in an appendix at the end of this book. Occasionally, I'll run half- and full-day hands-on workshops for creating comics. The schedule for my speaking engagements is also listed on the site.

We've also made the book's diagrams, screenshots, and other illustrations available under a Creative Common license for you to download and include in your own presentations. You can find these on Flickr at 🐘 www.flickr.com/photos/rosenfeldmedia/sets/.

FREQUENTLY ASKED QUESTIONS

What tools do I need?

To create a comic, you need a piece of paper and a pencil—nothing more. However, you do need to define a few things up front such as whom you're making the comic for and what you're trying to get your readers to do. Are you trying to get everyone on the same page? Get customers to sign up for your site? Communicate an internal process to your team? Educate someone on a topic? In addition to answering these questions, it will be helpful to know something about your characters through research and personas. Chapter 4 discusses these questions, while Chapter 7 covers a lot of the tools you can use.

What if I can't draw?

If you can draw a stick figure and a smiley face, you're already set. In Chapter 3, I explain just how little you need to get started, and I also give a few tips to help you feel more comfortable.

When should I use comics?

I don't advocate that comics should be used for everything, but there are scenarios where comics are appropriate at every point in a product cycle. Whether it's before you've started building a product and are still defining the requirements, in the midst of iterating on a product, or ready to launch a product, comics can have a place. Once you understand the strengths of comics and read about how others are using them, you'll be the best judge of when they're appropriate for your situation. You might want to check out Chapter 8 where I discuss some applications of comics.

How do I convince my client or team to use comics?

If you're reading this book, then I imagine I'm halfway to convincing you that comics are useful, but you may be wondering whether you'll be able to convince others to let you spend time drawing comics. This is probably the most common question I get when I talk about comics at conferences and workshops. That's why I've dedicated all of Chapter 9 to helping you. You'll be armed with data, examples of other companies using comics, and a few tips on how to communicate your goals.

CONTENTS

FOREWORD

And you who wish to represent by words the form of man...relinquish that idea. For the more minutely you describe, the more you will confine the mind of the reader, and the more you will keep him from the knowledge of the thing described. And so it is necessary to draw...

—Leonardo da Vinci, 1487

I think about this a lot. This is Leonardo, one of history's greatest thinkers, telling us that just talking is a bad way to describe an idea and often obscures its real essence. Leonardo is worth listening to. Here is the guy who invented the parachute, designed the helicopter, architected fortresses, engineered never-before-seen machines of every kind, and knew more about human anatomy than most doctors do today. And he also painted the Mona Lisa.

What would Leonardo think of the way we're taught to think today? He'd hate it. Modern education tells us we've got to become linear A-B-C specialists: if we want to engineer, we study calculus and computational fluid dynamics; if we want to design, we study human factors and heuristics; if we want to paint, we study painting. But Leonardo studies all these things—and he came up with new solutions to old problems every day. What did Leonardo know that we don't?

That is what Kevin's book is really about. If we want to fully describe an idea, we must both write it and *draw* it. Kevin calls this "comics," but I suspect that Kevin knows his term is a smokescreen. What Kevin is actually telling us—and *showing* us—is something far deeper and more powerful. It's this: drawing is the secret to thinking.

Language teachers, standardized test-creators, education experts, journalists, and most recruiters disagree. "Words," they say, "are the sign of intelligence. Just look at our greatest thinkers. Did they draw? No, they wrote! So learn your grammar, learn your five-paragraph essays, and shut up about your silly comics."

Anyone who tells you this is either lying, ignorant, or insane. Let's take a closer look at our greatest thinkers and see how they really thought. It comes as no surprise that many thought with pictures: Newton, Euclid, Descartes, Thomas Edison, Alexander Graham Bell, Einstein, Galileo, and Steve Jobs. They all drew. But we knew that.

But what about the writers, the philosophers, the historians—you know, the real thinkers? They didn't draw. Or did they?

WHO DREW?

LEONARDO DI VINCI drew the 1st parachute.

GALILEO understood the heavens by drawing charts.

ISAAC NEWTON drew schematics of physics + light

CHARLES DARWIN toyed with natural selection by drawing a tree.

ALEXANDER GRAHAM BELL drew diagrams to invent things.

THOMAS EDISON sketched everything.

SIGMUND FREUD drew maps of the psyche.

JRR TOLKIEN always drew as he wrote.

ALBERT EINSTEIN drew to show how his shoes didn't fit.

THEODORE GEISEL taught millions to read by drawing a cat (+ hat)

JACK KEROUAC wrote his 1st novel by drawing mandalas.

RICHARD FEYNMAN drew subatomic particles.

DONELLA MEADOWS invented systems thinking by drawing

ROLLIN KING founded Southwest Airlines with a sketch.

MICHAEL PORTER drew the 5 forces of competition

PRESIDENT OBAMA used to explain ideas with flowcharts.

STEVE JOBS ran meetings by mastering Venn Diagrams

JK ROWLING starts her writing by drawing a map.

The better question is WHO DIDN'T?

2012

continued on next page

Guess what: it turns out that most great thinkers drew—even though we're never taught that. Darwin first explored the idea of natural selection by drawing a tree. Jack Kerouac wrote his first novel by drawing his concept out as a mandala. J.R.R. Tolkien couldn't write without first drawing maps and portraits of his characters. Even J.K. Rowling just said that the first thing she did when she started to write her latest novel was to draw a map of the town in which it took place.

As Kevin says in the following pages:

> Through some invisible societal pressures, the kids learned that the label of "artist" carried with it some minimum level of talent. In reality, I'd suggest that you're an artist whether you call yourself one or not. So long as you can draw a stick figure, you're well on your way to being able to create simple stories that explain your ideas better than any well-crafted words could.

Kevin, you are so right! Thank you. Now show us what you mean.

—Dan Roam, author of *The Back of the Napkin* and *Blah Blah Blah*
San Francisco, October 2012

INTRODUCTION

I've been drawing comics for as long as I can remember. Like many comic book fans, when I was younger, I dreamed of becoming a professional comic book artist. But I was also extremely interested in computers, and comics quickly took a back seat as a hobby as I trained to become an engineer and later, a designer and product manager. In 2003, I decided to spend more time on my hobby by drawing a weekly webcomic with my former colleague Tom Chi. I wanted to make it funny, and to do so, I picked a topic I knew well—Human-Computer Interaction and user experience. That was the beginning of my intersection between my hobby and my professional life.

A couple of years later, Bill Buxton, who was working on his book *Sketching the User Experience*, met up with us at a CHI conference in Portland. Sketching was of course on his mind and during the course of our conversation, he asked if we'd ever considered using comics to aid in our designs. We hadn't, but the idea was intriguing. So intriguing, in fact, that I tried it on my very next project at Yahoo!. We presented about our experience to IA Summit the next year, just when Rosenfeld Media was getting started. Lou Rosenfeld, with his boundless optimism, suggested that the topic was worth writing a book about.

At this time, user experience was just finding its legs and a lot of energy was spent sharing tools of the trade: practical tools like wireframing, card sorting, user research, personas, and more. The idea of using comics to storyboard a use case wasn't new even then—there are examples from the 1980s and probably earlier of storyboards depicting how someone would use a hypothetical product. But it seemed that this technique was an inadvertent casualty of the field's maturation and many had forgotten the importance of sketching a story before any design work was done.

Since that first presentation, I was encouraged by those who used and adapted comics for various uses—at Adobe, eBay, Google, Adaptive Path, and many other organizations. I started seeing examples of comics in use in education, the military, and business books. The movie industry has understood the power of storyboarding for years, but now product creators were recognizing how they could be applied elsewhere.

Still, I saw a lot of hesitation and resistance. Mostly, people felt they couldn't draw or weren't confident they could convince their organization to invest time in comics. The goal of this book, then, is not to show off some brand new technique but rather to bring back an old tried-and-true technique and help you gain the confidence to use it in your work. I hope comics make their way into your already rich toolbox.

CHAPTER 1

Comics?!

HI! I'M *KEVIN*.

WHEN I WAS GROWING UP, I USED TO READ A LOT OF COMICS.

OK, I GUESS I STILL READ A LOT OF COMICS.

I ALSO STARTED PROGRAMMING WHEN I WAS 12...AND THAT LED TO MY CAREER NOW.

I'VE HELPED CREATE APPLICATIONS FOR WEBSITES AND PHONES.

SO I HAVE THESE TWO SIDES...

I NEVER IMAGINED THAT THEY WOULD EVER COME TOGETHER.

LET ME TELL YOU ABOUT THIS UNLIKELY MARRIAGE BETWEEN BUSINESS AND COMICS.

BEFORE THAT, A QUESTION FOR YOU:

WHAT DO YOU THINK OF WHEN I MENTION THE WORD *COMICS*?

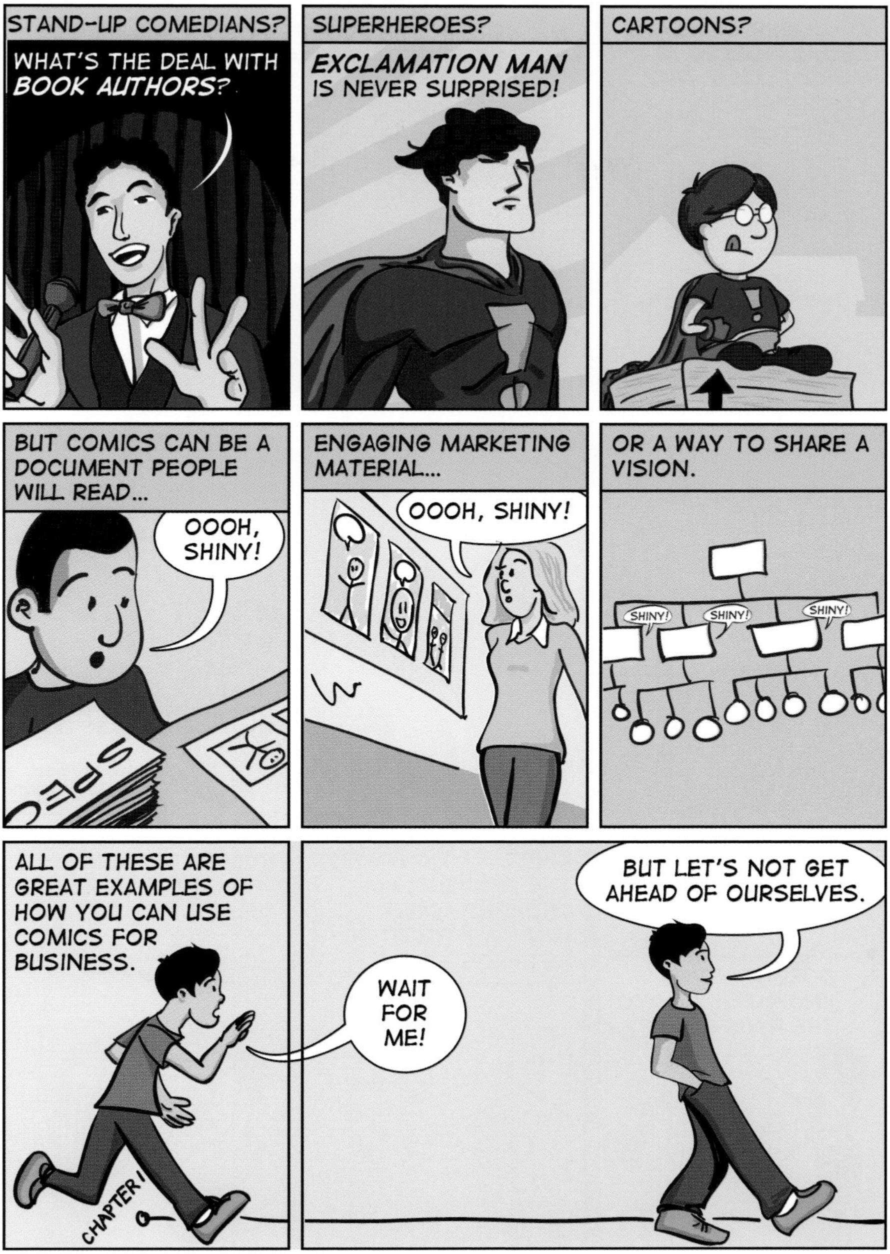
STAND-UP COMEDIANS?
WHAT'S THE DEAL WITH BOOK AUTHORS?
SUPERHEROES?
EXCLAMATION MAN IS NEVER SURPRISED!
CARTOONS?
BUT COMICS CAN BE A DOCUMENT PEOPLE WILL READ...
OOOH, SHINY!
SPEC
ENGAGING MARKETING MATERIAL...
OOOH, SHINY!
OR A WAY TO SHARE A VISION.
SHINY!
SHINY!
SHINY!
ALL OF THESE ARE GREAT EXAMPLES OF HOW YOU CAN USE COMICS FOR BUSINESS.
WAIT FOR ME!
BUT LET'S NOT GET AHEAD OF OURSELVES.
CHAPTER 1

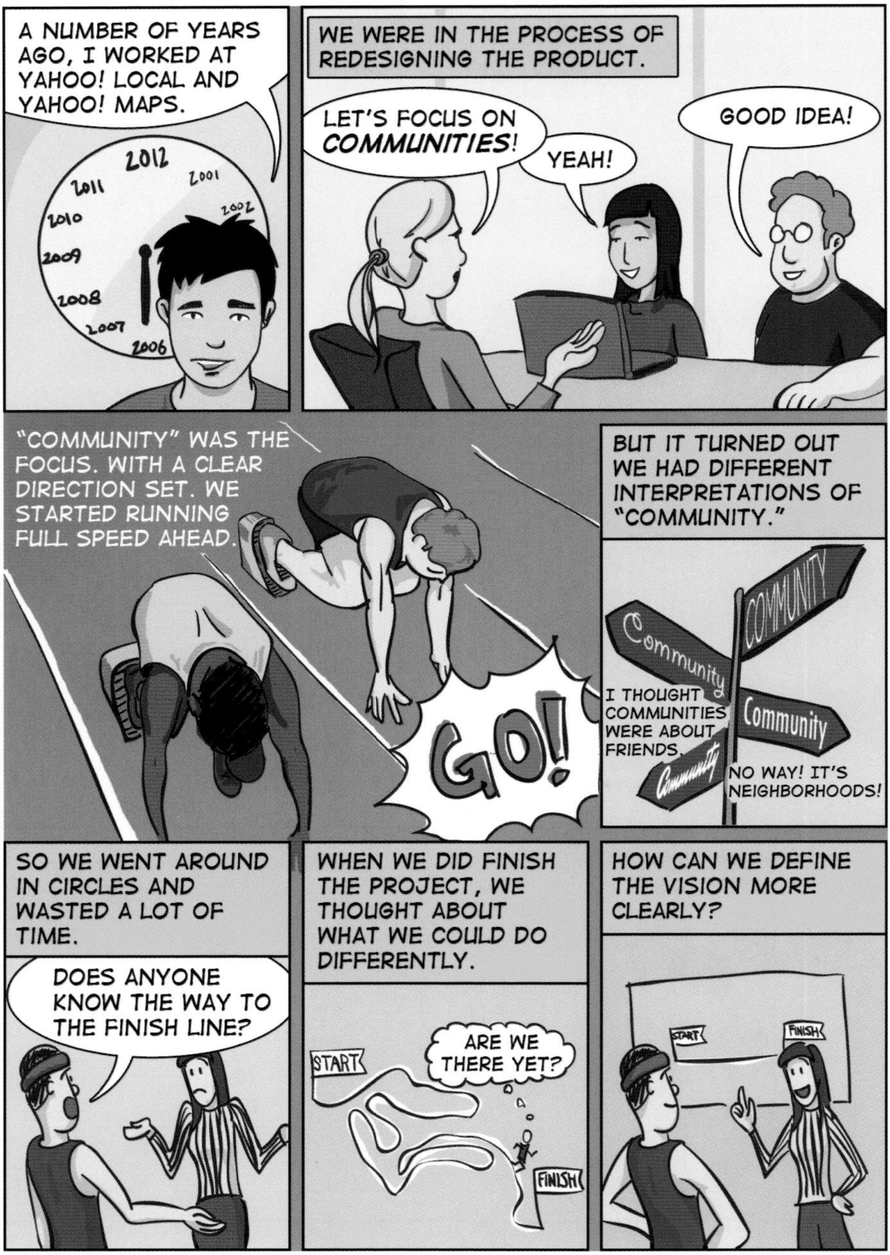
A NUMBER OF YEARS AGO, I WORKED AT YAHOO! LOCAL AND YAHOO! MAPS.
2012
2001
2011
2002
2010
2009
2008
2007
2006
WE WERE IN THE PROCESS OF REDESIGNING THE PRODUCT.
LET'S FOCUS ON COMMUNITIES!
YEAH!
GOOD IDEA!
"COMMUNITY" WAS THE FOCUS. WITH A CLEAR DIRECTION SET. WE STARTED RUNNING FULL SPEED AHEAD.
GO!
BUT IT TURNED OUT WE HAD DIFFERENT INTERPRETATIONS OF "COMMUNITY."
COMMUNITY
Community
Community
Community
I THOUGHT COMMUNITIES WERE ABOUT FRIENDS.
NO WAY! IT'S NEIGHBORHOODS!
SO WE WENT AROUND IN CIRCLES AND WASTED A LOT OF TIME.
DOES ANYONE KNOW THE WAY TO THE FINISH LINE?
WHEN WE DID FINISH THE PROJECT, WE THOUGHT ABOUT WHAT WE COULD DO DIFFERENTLY.
START
ARE WE THERE YET?
FINISH
HOW CAN WE DEFINE THE VISION MORE CLEARLY?
START
FINISH

REQUIREMENTS DIDN'T GET READ...

UH...I'LL FIND MY OWN WAY.

PROTOTYPES FOCUSED TOO MUCH ON DETAILS...

HMMM... WHICH SHOES ARE BETTER?

DO YOU KNOW WHERE YOU'RE GOING?

NO...

VIDEOS TOOK TOO LONG TO MAKE...

NONONO, WHAT'S YOUR *MOTIVATION?*

SO WE DECIDED TO TRY SOMETHING DIFFERENT. COMICS! LIKE THIS ONE...

I HATE THESE BUSINESS TRIPS. I WANT FOOD THAT ISN'T ROOM SERVICE. LET ME CHECK YAHOO! LOCAL...

SAN FRANCISCO...

LOOK AT ALL THESE GREAT RECOMMENDATIONS. THERE'S A MAP OF SAN FRANCISCO WITH THE LOCAL FAVORITES.

OH, I CAN SORT IT BY NEIGHBORHOOD! I THINK I'M IN THE FINANCIAL DISTRICT.

Refine Results
Neighborhood:
Financial District (405)
South of Market (750)
Union Square (441)
Pacific Heights (359)
Castro (251)

WE PRINTED AND EMAILED THE COMICS TO A LOT OF DIFFERENT PEOPLE.

WHAT THE~?

WE SHOWED THEM TO TEAMMATES...

TO EXECUTIVES...

AND EVEN TO POTENTIAL USERS!

THIS PART SEEMS COMPLICATED.

I HAVE TO ADMIT, EVEN I WAS SKEPTICAL TO BEGIN WITH.

BUT AT EVERY LEVEL, PEOPLE WERE REALLY ENGAGED.

AWESOME!

COOL!

THIS IS QUITE NEAT.

ESPECIALLY THE USERS.

AND THEN YOU DO THIS WITH THE *ZOOMUPABILITY!*

BY TELLING THE STORY OF THE PRODUCT, WE WERE ABLE TO ITERATE ON THE IDEA BEFORE WE STARTED BUILDING.

THAT PART DOESN'T SEEM VERY REALISTIC.

WHAT IF IT'S NOISY?

THE COMICS BROUGHT *USER EXPERIENCE* BACK INTO *USER EXPERIENCE DESIGN*.

INSTEAD OF FOCUS-ING ON A PRODUCT IN ISOLATION...

WE WERE ABLE TO FOCUS ON HOW THE PRODUCT WOULD BE USED IN CONTEXT.

AND EVERYONE WAS ON THE SAME PAGE.

SO WE ALWAYS KNEW WHICH WAY WE WERE GOING.

ALL IN ALL, WE WERE ABLE TO MOVE QUICKLY.

AND THAT WAS WHEN I REALIZED THAT COMICS HAD A PLACE IN THE BUSINESS WORLD.

MANY COMPANIES ARE STARTING TO USE COMICS...BUT IT'S STILL UNCOMMON.

I'M HOPING THIS BOOK WILL HELP YOU USE COMICS, TOO.

NO MATTER WHAT YOUR ROLE IS, YOU MAY FIND COMICS USEFUL FOR YOU.

IF YOU'RE A *LEADER* OF YOUR TEAM OR COMPANY, COMICS CAN HELP YOU DISTILL YOUR VISION.

THIS IS WHAT IT SHOULD BE LIKE TO USE OUR PRODUCTS.

FOR *MARKETING* AND *SALES*, COMICS HELP GET THE ATTENTION OF CUSTOMERS AND PARTNERS.

DESIGNERS AND *ENGINEERS* CAN USE COMICS TO CRYSTAL-LIZE THE PROBLEMS.

THIS PART SEEMS REALLY INEFFICIENT.

MAYBE WE CAN AUTOMATE IT.

USER RESEARCHERS CAN USE THE SAME STORY TO ANSWER THE QUESTION...

WOULD YOU OR ANYONE YOU KNOW ACTUALLY USE THIS?

PRODUCT MANAGERS CAN USE COMICS TO MAINTAIN FOCUS DURING DEVELOPMENT.

IN OTHER WORDS, NO MATTER WHAT YOUR ROLE IS...

COMICS MIGHT BE USEFUL TO...

YOU!

COMICS ARE A POWER-
FUL COMBINATION OF
WORDS AND PICTURES.

COMICS ARE A POWER-
FUL COMBINATION OF
WORDS AND PICTURES.

THEY COMMUNICATE
STORIES EFFICIENTLY.

THEY'RE INCREDIBLY
EXPRESSIVE.

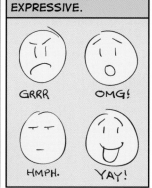

GRRR

OMG!

HMPH.

YAY!

AND ARE JUST
GENERALLY MORE
ENTERTAINING!

WHERE'S THE
SUNDAY FUNNIES?

NEWS

THE RESULT IS SOME-
THING PEOPLE WILL
ACTUALLY READ AND
UNDERSTAND.

I'M NOT SAYING
EVERYTHING SHOULD
BE DONE IN COMIC
FORM...

WHAT I HOPE TO GIVE
YOU IS ONE MORE
TOOL FOR YOUR
TOOLBOX, AND YOU
CAN CHOOSE WHEN
TO USE IT.

IN THIS BOOK, I'LL TALK ABOUT WHY YOU SHOULD USE COMICS AND WHEN TO USE THEM.

AND HOW YOU DON'T EVEN NEED TO KNOW HOW TO DRAW TO MAKE COMICS!

JUST AS LONG AS YOU CAN DRAW A STICK FIGURE!

I'LL START BY TELLING YOU ABOUT WHY COMICS ARE SO POWERFUL IN *CHAPTER 2*.

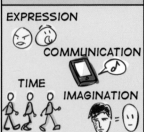

THEN IN *CHAPTER 3*, I'LL GO THROUGH SOME DRAWING BASICS.

CHAPTER 4 COVERS THE COMIC CREATION PROCESS AND THE FIRST STEP: DEFINING WHAT YOUR COMIC IS ABOUT.

CHAPTER 5 IS ABOUT WRITING THE COMIC BEFORE DRAWING IT.

AFTER THAT, THE NEXT STEP IS TO LAY OUT THE COMIC, COVERED IN *CHAPTER 6*.

THERE ARE SOME TOOLS IN *CHAPTER 7* TO HELP YOU MAKE COMICS MORE EASILY.

THROUGHOUT, WE'LL CREATE A COMIC TOGETHER FROM A HYPOTHETICAL EXAMPLE (BUT A REAL PRODUCT).

AFTERWARDS, I'LL TALK ABOUT WAYS YOU CAN USE YOUR COMIC IN *CHAPTER 8*.

VISION   MARKETING

RESEARCH

AND LASTLY, IN *CHAPTER 9*, I'LL TALK ABOUT SELLING COMICS IN YOUR ORGANIZATION.

COMICS?! HA!

YOU'LL ALSO HEAR FROM OTHER EXPERTS ALONG THE WAY.

commoncraft

nForm.

JOHNNY BUNKO

JUST AS I HAVE TWO SIDES, EACH CHAPTER WILL HAVE TWO FORMATS.

THE FIRST WILL BE A COMIC SUMMARY OF THE CHAPTER.

FOLLOWED BY MORE DETAILED TEXT COVERING THE TOPIC.

Chapter 2

SO YOU'LL HAVE TWO WAYS TO READ THE BOOK!

WELL, I GUESS WE MAY AS WELL GET STARTED...

LET'S GO!

CHAPTER 2

Properties of Comics

COMICS HAVE HAD A LONG-STANDING WORLDWIDE CULTURAL IMPACT ACROSS ALL AGES.

IN JAPAN, COMICS (OR *MANGA*) COVER TOPICS INCLUDING SPORTS, ROMANCE, BUSINESS, AND MATH.

COMICS SUCH AS *THE ADVENTURES OF TIN TIN* AND *ASTERIX* HAVE BEEN TRANSLATED INTO OVER 80 LANGUAGES!

HELLO

BONJOUR

NI HAO

THERE'S NOTHING WRONG WITH COMICS THAT ARE "JUST FOR KIDS"...

WHAT?

BUT RECENTLY, A SURGE OF COMICS TACKLING MORE SERIOUS SUBJECTS HAS EMERGED AND SHOWCASE THE POWER OF THE MEDIUM.

FUN HOME   MAUS   CANCER VIXEN

COMICS MAY TAKE MANY FORMS. *COMIC STRIPS* FIT IN LESS THAN A PAGE, LIKE THE SUNDAY FUNNIES.

WHAT WE CALL *COMIC BOOKS* ARE OFTEN MORE LIKE MAGAZINES IN SIZE.

WHILE COHESIVE STORYLINES ARE OFTEN COLLECTED OR RELEASED AS BOUND BOOKS CALLED *GRAPHIC NOVELS*.

WHATEVER THE FORMAT, THERE'S SOME COMMON VOCABUARY USED IN COMICS THAT I'LL BE USING IN THIS BOOK.

THIS BOX I'M IN IS CALLED A PANEL.

WHILE THIS SPACE IS A *GUTTER*.

THE *DIALOGUE* DESCRIBES THE WORDS I'M SAYING.

DIALOGUE HAPPENING OUTSIDE OF THE PANEL IS CALLED *OFF-PANEL* DIALOGUE.

THE THING HOLDING MY DIALOGUE IS CALLED A *SPEECH BUBBLE*.

THOUGH YOU CAN JUST USE A LINE IF YOU WANT.

MEANWHILE, BACK IN GOTHAM CITY...

THE TEXT UP TOP IS CALLED A *CAPTION* AND IS USED FOR NARRATION.

THAT'S IT! NOW WE CAN TALK *ABOUT* COMICS.

LET'S TALK ABOUT *WHY* COMICS ARE POWERFUL. I BREAK IT UP INTO FOUR CATEGORIES.

1. COMMUNICATION

IF COMICS ARE SEQUENTIAL ART, THEN CAVE PAINTINGS MIGHT BE THE FIRST FORM OF COMICS.

COMICS ARE A UNIVERSAL LANGUAGE. ITS VOCABULARY INCLUDES MORE THAN WORDS.

A FEW LINES CAN INDICATE NEGATIVE EMOTION, CURSING, SHAKING, AND MORE!

2. IMAGINATION: COMICS ALLOW YOU TO ABSTRACT DETAILS AND ONLY SHOW WHAT'S IMPORTANT.

PROBABLY KEVIN

COULD BE ANYONE

WITH LESS DETAIL, READERS CAN CONNECT TO CHARACTERS, PLACES, AND EVEN INTERFACES HOWEVER THEY WANT.

3. EXPRESSION: THE COMBINATION OF WORDS AND PICTURES AMPLIFY THE MEANING OF BOTH.

I'M SORRY

I'M SORRY

THANK YOU

THANK YOU

AND YOU CAN SIMPLY AND CLEARLY EXPRESS EMOTIONS BY JUST CHANGING THE EYE-BROWS AND MOUTH.

BODY LANGUAGE IS ALSO POWERFUL. THE WAY THE BODY LEANS TELLS A LOT TO THE READER.

4. TIME: FINALLY, COMICS ARE GREAT AT CONVEYING THE PASSAGE OF TIME.

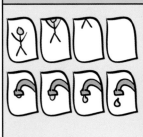

BLANK PANELS OR REPEATED PANELS SHOW TIME PASSING.

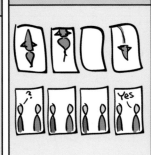

AND... TIME PASSES... EVEN IN THE SAME PANEL!

The word "comics" carries many connotations. In North America, the word is often synonymous with "cartoons" and considered to be something for children. For example, cartoons might be associated with *Batman, Superman, Spider-Man*, and *X-Men* or with *Garfield, Calvin & Hobbes*, and *The Family Circus*.

Merriam–Webster defines comics (or comic) as:

- comedian (a stand-up comic)

- the comic element

- a: comic strip, b: comic book, c (plural): the part of a newspaper devoted to comic strips

and subsequently defines a comic strip as:

- a group of cartoons in narrative sequence

While Sunday comics are a defining part of many people's experience with comics, it only represents a fraction of what comics are. In my opinion, this definition is indicative of how comics are underappreciated as an art form and a communication medium. In fact, comics have had a long-standing worldwide cultural impact across all ages.

Comics Around the World

In Japan, comics are known as *manga*. They are seen as a popular and mainstream form of entertainment, covering a wide variety of topics, including sports, fantasy, romance, business, and education. The audience demographic is just as broad as the subject matter.

When best-selling author Daniel Pink was living in Tokyo, he noticed how prevalent manga was. As an experiment, he attempted to walk a city block without seeing somebody holding or reading a comic book—and failed. He was so inspired by this medium that he decided to write his next business book, *The Adventures of Johnny Bunko*, in comic form. In Chapter 8, "Applying Comics," we'll hear more from Daniel about his book and why comics worked for him.

Comics are quite popular in Europe as well. The Belgian series *Adventures of Tin Tin* and the French series *Asterix* were so popular that they were both translated into over 80 languages. Their longevity is equally impressive: *Tin Tin* first appeared in 1929, and its collections are still being reprinted today, while *Asterix* has been around since 1959 and is still running!

Comics for Young and Old

It may surprise you as it did me that a comic book was named *Time Magazine*'s Book of the Year. There's nothing wrong with comics that are "just for kids"; I still thoroughly enjoy comic strips such as *Foxtrot* or *Calvin & Hobbes,* as well as the occasional superhero comic or movie. But in the last decade, a surge of comics tackling more serious subjects has emerged that can only be described as art. The *New York Times* recognized this trend by starting a Graphic Books Best Seller List category in 2009.

Even if you don't end up drawing a single stick figure, I hope you check out some of these masterpieces. They can illustrate the power of the medium far better than I ever could and will entertain you at the same time. Their subject matter is as diverse as their art styles:

- *Fun Home: A Family Tragicomic*, a memoir by Alison Bechdel, deals with sexual orientation, suicide, and complex family relationships. It's the book that made the *New York Times Best Seller List* before there was a graphic books category and also won Book of the Year.

- *300* and *Sin City* are two comics by American writer and artist Frank Miller. One is a violent fictional retelling of the Battle of Thermopylae and the other is a *film noir* style thriller about murder, betrayal, and corruption. Both are incredibly violent and were turned into equally visually stunning films.

- *Persepolis* is an autobiographical series about author Marjane Satrapi's experiences growing up in Iran.

- *Transmetropolitan* is a 10-volume series by British writer Warren Ellis. It may not be as well known as the others I've listed here, but it's a great example of comics being used as political commentary.

- *Blankets*, another autobiographical tale, is an impressive 592 pages about first love, religion, and adolescence by Craig Thompson.

- *Bone*, by Jeff Smith, is perhaps the first series that has managed to properly recapture the purity of Disney characters, but like *Harry Potter* and other popular children's books, it weaves in deeper themes and emotions that can be appreciated by older readers.

Comic Formats

So what's the difference between a comic book and a graphic novel? Or between a comic strip and a cartoon? Comics can take many forms and depending on how they are bound and distributed, a different name is used to refer to them.

The comics you find in newspapers are referred to as *comic strips.* They usually have fewer than a dozen boxes and are often self-contained. We don't usually refer to them as *cartoons* because that confuses them with the animated cartoons. Besides, Saturday is for cartoons, and Sunday is the day for comic strips!

Today, what we call *comic books* really aren't books at all. They tend to be the size and format of a magazine. These comic books are often released weekly as part of an ongoing series.

For popular and cohesive storylines, comic books are sometimes collected and reprinted as one bound book. Recently, it's become more popular to simply release them directly in bound book form. In either case, these bound comic books are often referred to as *graphic novels.*

Anatomy of a Comic

Like any subject matter, comics have a set of common vocabulary words to refer to their components. Thankfully, the list is small and reasonably descriptive with no gratuitous use of foreign languages (see Figure 2.1). For example, if this book were about dance, you'd be learning about how a dance for two isn't a "dance for two" but a *pas de deux.*

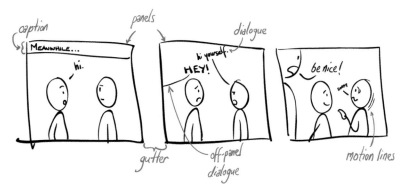

FIGURE 2.1
The anatomy of comics.

Comics generally consist of a series of boxes to show the progression of the story. Each of these boxes that contains the art and words is called a *panel.* The border itself is sometimes called the *frame,* but the two words end up being used interchangeably quite often. I'll be using panels to describe each box. A panel also isn't necessarily rectangular in shape.

The space between two or more panels is referred to as the *gutter.* It's rare that anything goes here at all.

The text coming out of characters' mouths is referred to as *dialogue*. (I guess we do use some French words!) A simple line is enough to show where the words are coming from, but if you want to add a bubble around it, these are called *speech bubbles*. If the dialogue or some other action is coming from somewhere outside of what's visible in the panel, we call that *off-panel*.

Motion lines refer to lines that don't actually represent anything physical but convey something moving (or in this example, shaking).

Finally, when we talk about the *caption*, we're referring to the narrative text that typically resides near the top of the panel. The caption is where, "It was a dark and stormy night…" or, "Meanwhile, in Gotham City…" might appear.

NOTE REALLY, WHAT ARE COMICS?

The Eisner Awards are the comic industry's version of the Academy Awards. It's named after Will Eisner, the American comics writer and artist, who also wrote the book *Comics and Sequential Art.* His book title was also the first time that comics were described as sequential art, which is really what a comic is. Comics are the juxtaposition of words and art placed in a sequence.

Comics can be a single panel like *The Far Side;* a comic strip consisting of 2–6 panels, such as Calvin & Hobbes; a traditional magazine-size comic book like *X-Men;* or a full-length graphic novel, such as *Blankets.*

The Four Properties of Comics

When you go to a website, you don't necessarily need to have design training to appreciate good design. As a Web designer, I appreciate everyone's feedback on my designs, regardless of their background. However, because I do have experience and training for designing these experiences, I also have a pretty good grasp of *why* a site is well designed or not.

I know how the use of colors can impact the emotional connection, how the use of different fonts and font sizes can be used to differentiate sections, and how to organize the information so that visitors can find what they want to find.

That doesn't mean you need a degree in design to create better websites, though. If you bought a book on visual design basics, you'd learn a lot of the principles I just mentioned and could probably describe why a design works or doesn't work better than most people. You can do a lot with just a little bit of theory.

Here's another example: We know we need to eat and drink to stay alive; our body tells us this, and we don't need to know how our body works to appreciate that. At the other end of the spectrum, you could study for years to be a doctor who understood all the intricacies of the human body and how every chemical affected you, but that would be pretty extreme if all you wanted to do was improve your nutrition. Instead, you could learn some basics about processed foods, cholesterol levels, calorie counts, and vitamin needs. This relatively small amount of knowledge could get you a long way.

That's the level of theory I'd like to share with you. You might know that comics are a compact and engaging way to communicate to your audience but not quite why. By understanding a few basic properties of comics, you can create much better comics yourself.

I will organize the properties of comics here into four categories: communication, imagination, expression, and time. These properties are not all unique to comics, but they are areas in which comics excel.

Communication

Will Eisner calls comics *sequential art*. Interpreted literally, that's "art that tells a story by putting a number of them in sequence." By that definition, the earliest comics came in the form of hieroglyphics or even cave paintings, as shown in Figure 2.2.

Comics existed over 10,000 years ago!

FIGURE 2.2
Prehistoric comics.

Perhaps you may be thinking, "But wait, Kevin. Didn't you just say that comics are the juxtaposition of words and illustrations? Cave paintings clearly don't have any words."

That is precisely one of the strengths of comics that many people don't recognize. Hidden within comics is a universal language. That language is represented by iconic imagery, body language, and facial expressions that transcend words.

Here's an example of such imagery. Back at Yahoo!, my design manager Tom Wailes owned a T-shirt, which had a picture similar to the one in Figure 2.3. Aside from being a champion for the comics method within Yahoo!, he also had impeccable fashion sense.

FIGURE 2.3
What's that doggie
doing?

What is the dog doing in the picture? Everybody I've shown this picture to knows the answer. A few have some alternate answers. My favorite was, "Maybe it's a sales dog, and it's talking out of its ass."

It's not surprising that you recognize what the dog is doing, but what surprised Tom was how his two-year-old son, who had never read a comic book in his life, laughed at the shirt and indicated that he understood the dog was passing gas.

Tom's son might be a prodigy, but this comprehension wasn't proof of it. I explained to Tom that comics have a vocabulary that doesn't even require language. In fact, many of its symbols could be considered a language of their own that requires no teaching or explanation.

When there's a speech bubble, even an empty one, we know it indicates a sound. When we see action lines, we know they represent movement. When the shapes of those lines change, we can interpret emotions such as anger.

One of the reasons that comics like *Asterix* and *Adventures of Tin Tin* translate so well is because they use the same methods to show pain or joy or anger across all of the translations, changing only the words in the comic. If I picked up a French copy of *Asterix*, I would find the same art as I would in any other language. Even when they represent characters cursing, they use symbols to illustrate the emotions, as I've done in Figure 2.4.

FIGURE 2.4
Speech bubbles, motion lines, and angry squiggles!

Imagination

In the book *Understanding Comics*, Scott McCloud discusses the idea of abstraction. He describes how in comics, you can abstract details in characters so as to allow the reader to bring his own imagination into the story. To illustrate this, I'm going to borrow an example from Scott's book.

I've drawn three versions of myself in Figure 2.5 with differing levels of detail. At one end, the simple stick-figure rendition could be interpreted as not resembling me at all or possibly resembling anyone. The lack of detail makes it look like nobody *and* everybody. On the far right, the drawing is much more detailed and leaves little room for interpretation as to who is being represented.

FIGURE 2.5
Varying details of Kevin.

By reducing the amount of detail in a drawing, you can encourage your reader to relate personally to what's being presented. The more detailed and specific a drawing, the more concretely defined it is. You can draw a bridge that looks like a bridge, or you can make it very plainly the Golden Gate Bridge. When it's just a bridge, the reader might associate a bridge they're familiar with in their mind and thus create a more personal connection to your comic.

The lack of detail can be accomplished in the art by using fewer lines. But you can also remove details by being symbolic instead of literal. For example, you could use animals instead of people—like a talking rabbit or a hapless coyote.

When we watch cartoons like *Bugs Bunny* and *Road Runner*, we feel a certain connection to the characters. We laugh at the plight of Wile E. Coyote, but also sympathize with him. These characters are drawn simply and don't try to photo-realistically portray rabbits and coyotes; we would have a lot of trouble connecting with that! In addition to being simplified drawings, though, they're also abstracted by not being human characters. They're not old or young, black or white. They are simply characters. For Road Runner and Wile E. Coyote, the characters are abstracted even further by having no voice. Without a voice, you can't presume anything based on their accents.

The viewer isn't consciously thinking, "I'm just like Wile E. Coyote. I can never seem to get things right," or "Road Runner is just like my friend Peter!" Nevertheless, they're likely to feel a deeper connection to the characters because subconsciously they can apply their own experiences to fill in the abstractions.

You don't have to use the same level of detail across the whole comic, either. By varying the detail of various elements, you can call attention to particular aspects and help guide the reader's imagination.

A common practice in manga is to draw a very detailed background with fairly simplistic characters. The effect is twofold. First, the characters pop out of the detailed background, creating an effective contrast that guides the reader's focus to the characters. Second, the detailed background makes the setting very clear while the character remains abstract, allowing for better reader-to-character immersion, as shown in Figure 2.6. Scott McCloud eloquently calls this "one to see, one to be."

FIGURE 2.6
A detailed background leaves no room for interpretation, but the character stands out with its lack of detail.

The practice of reducing detail isn't just restricted to the art. We can also be deliberately vague when conveying user interfaces or processes in our comics.

We learned this when we were creating our comics at Yahoo! Local. In one particular panel, we wanted to illustrate that our character, Dana, was searching through Yahoo! Local (see Figure 2.7). How the search was performed was unimportant; we simply wanted to convey how Dana got to the subsequent page.

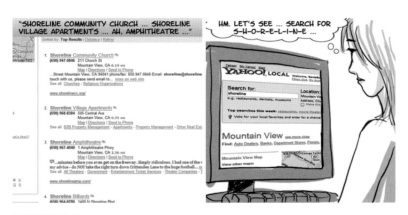

FIGURE 2.7
Yahoo! Local comic where Dana is searching for restaurants.

Because the search results page already existed, we thought it would be easier to use a screenshot. In hindsight, the outcome should have been quite predictable. Readers focused on the design and content of the search results page more than the story itself.

Once we discovered this problem, we reduced the level of detail so the reader saw only what was necessary to understand context. We included the site's logo, a search box, and the location in large print. The fact that the screenshot wasn't entirely accurate wasn't an issue—just as the fact that a face is only a caricature wasn't an issue.

Then we took the idea of simplification even further by removing the view of the screen entirely, as shown in Figure 2.8.

FIGURE 2.8
Showing interface options without showing the screen.

In both of these versions, we can't see the screen that the character is viewing, but we reveal just the right amount of interface to communicate the pertinent elements. In the second iteration, the interface elements are handdrawn, making the elements informal and even more concise. Keeping the interface within the same artistic style as the rest of the comic also made it less jarring for the reader.

Recognizing how much to abstract away requires some amount of experimentation and practice. For the moment, simply remember the power that abstraction in comics gives you.

Expression

A picture is worth a thousand words, but in comics, pictures can be used to give words richer meaning. If we consider the two phrases, "I'm sorry" and "thank you," they appear to be fairly objective statements (see Figure 2.9). One is an apology, while the other is a signal of appreciation.

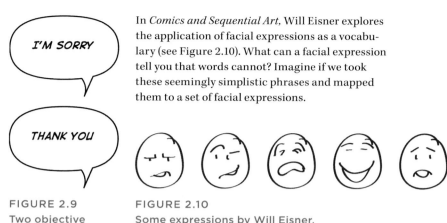

In *Comics and Sequential Art,* Will Eisner explores the application of facial expressions as a vocabulary (see Figure 2.10). What can a facial expression tell you that words cannot? Imagine if we took these seemingly simplistic phrases and mapped them to a set of facial expressions.

FIGURE 2.9
Two objective statements.

FIGURE 2.10
Some expressions by Will Eisner.

The same words, expressed with the same font, emphasis, and dialogue bubbles, now carry an added layer of meaning, as shown in Figure 2.11.

Looking at the words with their added context, the phrases might be considered reluctant, taunting, heartfelt, or insincere.

FIGURE 2.11
Expressions change the meaning of the words.

When we consider our face-to-face interaction with other people, the fact that facial expressions add additional meaning may come as no surprise. What is perhaps more unexpected is how little one needs to show to convey meaningful facial expressions.

It turns out you can illustrate emotions by modifying only the eyebrows and the mouth (see Figure 2.12). Between these two facial features, a whole myriad of expressions can be represented.

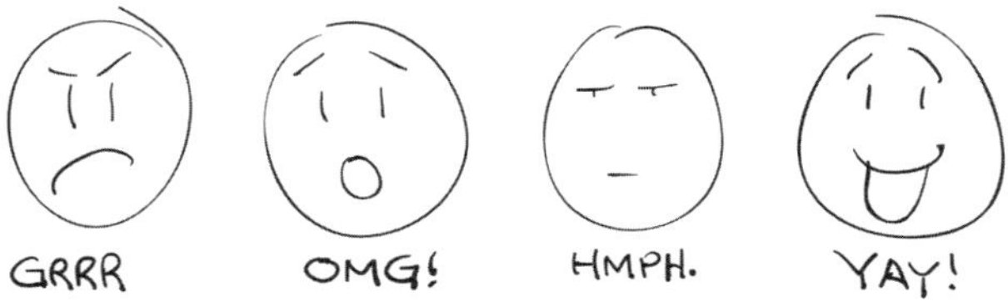
GRRR
OMG!
HMPH.
YAY!

FIGURE 2.12
Just change the eyebrows and the mouth.

In fact, the character *EVE* in Pixar's movie *Wall•E* illustrates that you can still communicate emotion without any mouth or eyebrows, but simply by shaping the eyes (see Figure 2.13).

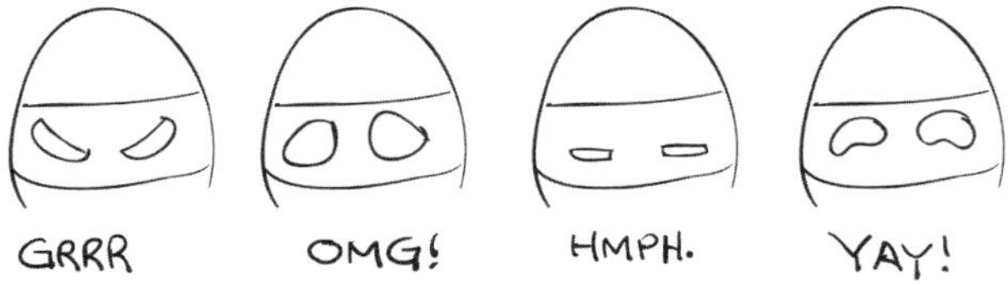
GRRR
OMG!
HMPH.
YAY!

FIGURE 2.13
Just the eyes can be enough.

Of course, both *Wall•E* and *EVE* have another characteristic to help communicate emotion—their body language.

When a person leans forward, it implies dominance, confidence, or intimidation. Leaning backward can communicate a need for distance, insecurity, or even fear. Drawing body language isn't as hard as you might think. Even a stick figure has body language.

Take a look at these drawings in Figure 2.14 of a person at a computer before and after waiting for a long time for the system to respond. While the eyebrows and mouth already communicate displeasure, the person's hunched posture and the hand against the chin emphasize frustration and impatience. The posture could be interpreted as saying, "I've been waiting so long I can't even hold my head up anymore."

By understanding how a few lines can affect the message being communicated, we can convey an incredible amount of information.

FIGURE 2.14
Body language can say a lot with very little.

Sketch, Sketch, Sketch

While comics have many incredible properties to them, even just the act of sketching can be beneficial. Joshua Brewer, author and co-founder of the blog "52 Weeks of UX" and designer at Twitter, wrote this piece on the benefits of sketching.

I've heard it so many times: "I can't sketch a stick figure to save my life."

Some people are afraid of showing their drawing to others. They think they'll be ridiculed if their sketch looks like it was drawn by a five-year-old.

In truth, it doesn't matter if you are good at sketching. The less formal the sketch, the better. In fact, avoid the urge to use a pencil as it leaves too much room for you to ponder, erase, re-draw, second-guess....

But a permanent marker, *now you're talking*. A nice big, fat Sharpie is the perfect tool because it requires you to really think through your idea before you put the pen to the paper. "What if it doesn't work or the layout's all wrong? " Great! Grab a new piece of paper and start from where you left off, having learned something valuable in a matter of minutes.

The sketch is not the end goal. The end goal of the drawing process is what you learn *while* sketching. So don't worry if you can't sketch. In fact, if you're too good, you might just fool yourself into thinking your sketch is a *deliverable*. It's not. The real value of sketching is that it allows you to explore and refine ideas in a quick, iterative, and visual manner with little overhead or learning curve. Rapid ideation around flow and interaction, layout and hierarchy, can be quickly established, rearranged, or discarded wholesale—all without ever touching a computer.

One added benefit to sketching your ideas is the ability to share, collaborate, and improve upon an idea. Show a stakeholder the sketch and then encourage that person to mark it up. You can even give them the red pen and let them revel in the power!

In the end, you will gain a deeper understanding of the problem you are trying to solve, and a head start on implementing a great design!

Time

When you try to describe how long something takes, how do you express it? You might use specific terms such as, "I was stuck in traffic for an hour!" You can also describe time in more generic terms like, "It took ages." Another way to describe the passage of time is by describing the action in more detail. For example, you might say, "All the cars were moving really slowly."

Comics convey time a bit differently. With words, you can describe exactly how long you were stuck in traffic. With a movie, you can actually experience the passage of time through time passing in the movie itself—although it wouldn't be a terribly fun movie to watch a traffic jam for an hour. With comics, you can still use words to express time explicitly, but you also have many other tools at your disposal.

One simple way to illustrate time and motion in comics is to treat the comic like a book version of an animation. Each panel then acts like a frame in the animation. Here's the story of a girl who can jump really high in Figure 2.15.

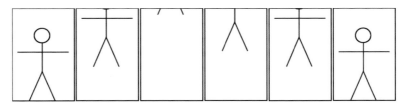

FIGURE 2.15
Jump! Comics as animation.

With this example, we can visualize the character jumping. We can't tell exactly how long the jump is, but the relative height of the jump and our own understanding of gravity give us a rough idea. In the same way that we use our own experiences to fill in the blanks for characters, we picture the jump and the time elapsed in our mind. The exact amount of time doesn't matter in this case. Instead, we've communicated a very simple story that the reader can actually experience.

When we treat comics like a print version of animation, each panel is representative of the same unit of time. We automatically imagine that the time between each panel is the same from one panel to the next. This animation is also a great example of how the gutter isn't just empty space; it's also the space where time passes.

Let's play with time a little bit in Figure 2.16. If each panel represents the same unit of time, what if we just insert a few more panels that are completely empty in the middle of the comic?

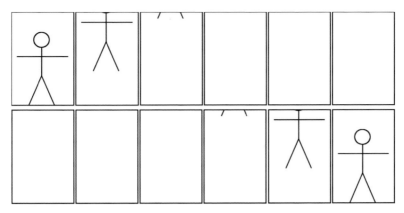

FIGURE 2.16
Blank panels can mean time passing.

The effect is clear. Just by inserting a few blank panels, we've given the impression that more time has elapsed. Either the girl is now jumping really high or a spaceship has abducted our heroine. Even though nothing is happening in the panel itself, the reader assumes time is elapsing and the character is somewhere off-panel, above the field of vision, only to return to the ground much later—perhaps after the alien abductors rejected her.

But you don't necessarily have to add multiple panels to show that a lot of time has passed. Sometimes, just extending the size of a panel can suggest the same effect, as in Figure 2.17. Equally, making a very narrow panel can suggest a very short amount of time (see Figure 2.18).

FIGURE 2.17
Longer panels represent more time passing.

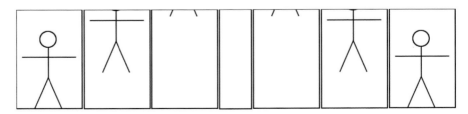

FIGURE 2.18
A narrow panel has the opposite effect.

In the examples I've shown so far, time has been represented by blank spaces, either in the gutters or the panels. You can also show time passing through repetition. Have you ever asked someone a question, only to have that person stare at you blankly for a few seconds before responding? Comics are really phenomenal at portraying these little moments, and it's dead easy to do. To show a pause in a scene, you can just repeat the scene for another panel like the one shown in Figure 2.19.

FIGURE 2.19
Repeating a panel to create a pause.

The contents of the panel matter, too. With the jumping girl, we associate a certain timeframe because of our understanding of gravity. If the girl were wearing a cape instead, the comic would suggest the girl was a superhero and had perhaps flown away. How long it took before she returned would not be as obvious then.

That means we could draw the same number of panels, at the same size, and still change the perceived time by changing what's in the panel. A dripping sink like the one in Figure 2.20, for example, would suggest a more drawn-out time sequence.

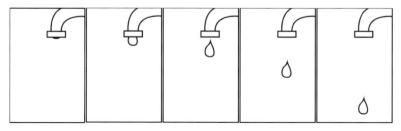

FIGURE 2.20
Changing the content of the comic also impacts time perception.

Sometimes, you may want to be a bit more explicit about how much time is passing. You can do this by explicitly stating the time as we do in conversation. A character could easily say, "Traffic took an hour!" Alternatively, you could use a reference object to show a lot of time had passed.

In the BBC rendition of Jane Austen's *Pride & Prejudice*, there's a scene where Mr. Darcy is sitting at his desk, getting ready to write a heartfelt letter to Lizzie. The scene fades out and then back in to another cut of Mr. Darcy, still sitting at his desk struggling to come up with the right words. Behind Mr. Darcy, we notice a candle, which has burnt significantly more since the time he first sat down. The viewer has no explicit indication of how long he'd been sitting there, but the candle suggests the duration.

The same technique can be applied to comics. You can show a scene with a clock in the background and then show the same scene with a later time on the clock, similar to Figure 2.21. Or you can show a scene during the day and then the same at night.

FIGURE 2.21
Reference objects can indicate time passing.

You can see how almost every aspect of a comic allows you to play with time. I feel it's one of the more fun aspects of the medium. While I've shown a number of different ways that comics can uniquely communicate the passage of time, these examples are only a small sampling of what is possible. Much like poems, music, or even sentence structures, comics can use the basic structures and foundations, but more advanced and experienced practitioners of the medium can be more creative and can find novel ways to communicate time and motion.

I encourage you to experiment with these tricks as you create your comics. Once you've gotten a grasp of how time works in comics, you can start trying some really crazy time bending (see Figure 2.22).

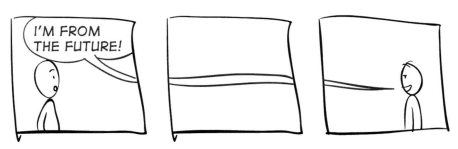

FIGURE 2.22
The webcomic XKCD plays with time.

The Google Chrome Comic

In 2008, Google decided to launch a new Web browser called *Google Chrome*. The market for browsers was already crowded with Internet Explorer, Mozilla Firefox, and Apple Safari battling for market share. Adding to the confusion was the fact that Google and Mozilla had a close business relationship.

In fact, Google had a lot of good but rather technical reasons for creating a new browser. They were trying to remedy a lot of limitations with modern browsers.

One example of the problems they were trying to solve, as explained by a Google engineer:

"Once you have JavaScript executing, it's going to keep going, and the browser can't do anything else until JavaScript returns control to the browser. So developers write APIs that are asynchronous and every now and then the browser locks up because JavaScript is hung up on something."

Imagine 30, 50, or even 100 pages of this. Even the best of geeks would be hard pressed to find the time. The team recognized how important it was to explain why they were building Chrome so their users didn't simply compare features but needed an accessible medium.

Anna-Christina Douglas was the product marketer for Google Chrome. She explains the problem they were trying to solve, "We wanted to get the technical story out there and help people understand why we were doing it in a clear and digestible way. If we only did a white paper, nobody was going to read it."

"We were trying to create something that helped focus the story on the technology innovations and not the browser wars or feature comparison. Our goal was to explain this to the technical bloggers and tech-savvy audience who would be interested in one level deeper than features but who wouldn't read engineering notes and extrapolate the story from there. At the same time, we didn't want to dumb it down and alienate those who would read the white paper so the comic didn't water down what the technology was doing."

"Using comics (see Figure 2.23) gave us a way to create something digestible and playful. We have these things called Tech Talks where an engineer gets up and talks about a product. The comic was similar to that. It felt in line with the Google brand."

FIGURE 2.23
Sample of the Google Chrome comic.

When it came time to launch the product, a shipping error caused the comic to leak a day before the announcement. As it turned out, by having the comic released first, everyone focused on the comic before the product. By the time Google Chrome actually launched, most of the press and enthusiastic audience already understood the motivation and innovation behind the browser.

"It was a happy accident."

Summary

Comics are a medium that combines the strengths of words and pictures to create something new and powerful. Today, they're breaking out of the stereotype of spandex and Sunday Funnies into a true form of communication and expression.

Panels, gutters, dialogue, and captions are the components that make a comic, and there are four properties of comics that make them special:

- **Communication:** Comics are a universal form of communication, more easily understood and older than words.

- **Imagination:** You can abstract the unimportant details in a comic, encouraging the reader to focus on the areas of the story that are most important.

- **Expression:** By combining words with simple facial expressions and body gestures, comics can provide more meaning than either words or pictures.

- **Time:** The use of white space, panel size, and reference points provides many creative ways to express time in comics.

When you use comics to communicate an idea, remember these four properties to maximize the impact you can have.

You Don't Need to Be an Artist

HOW MANY OF YOU THINK YOU'RE AN ARTIST?

IF I ASKED YOU WHEN YOU WERE 4 YEARS OLD, WHAT WOULD YOU HAVE SAID?

THE TRUTH IS, IF YOU CAN DRAW A FEW BASIC SHAPES, YOU CAN MAKE USEFUL COMICS.

FOR EXAMPLE, I BET YOU CAN DRAW A SMILEY FACE...

AND A STICK FIGURE! WITH A FEW MORE BASICS, YOU CAN DO MUCH MORE.

YOU CAN USE THE SIZE OF A HEAD TO HELP MEASURE THE PROPORTIONS OF A BODY. BUT DON'T GET HUNG UP ON BEING EXACT. MORE IMPORTANT IS HOW THE BODY IS POSITIONED.

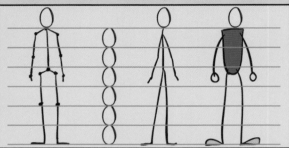

LEANING FORWARD SHOWS INTEREST, CONCENTRATION, OR ANGER.

LEANING BACK CAN MEAN FEAR, APPRE-HENSION, SURPRISE, OR REJECTION.

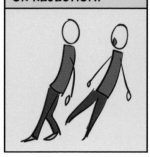

WHERE YOU PUT THE ARMS CAN TELL A LOT, TOO!

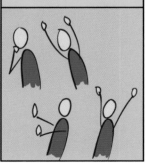

ONCE YOU GET MORE COMFORTABLE, YOU CAN START ADDING DETAILS.

STARTING FROM A STICK FIGURE, YOU CAN ADD A RECTANGLES FOR THE BODY.

AND THEN ADD SOME LIMBS!

AS I MENTIONED, FACES ARE VERY EXPRESSIVE. TRY JUST CHANGING THE MOUTH...

AND THEN THE JUST THE EYEBROWS.

LIKE THE BODY, FACES HAVE PROPORTIONS AND GUIDELINES. IF YOU DRAW AN OVAL...

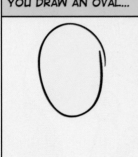

AND THEN A CROSS THROUGH THE MIDDLE...

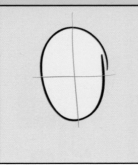

YOU HAVE THE POSITION OF THE EYES!

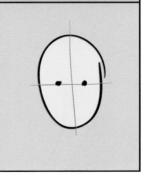

IF YOU SPLIT THE BOTTOM HALF INTO THIRDS, THAT'S THE MOUTH AND NOSE!

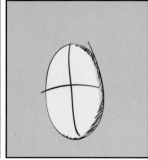

NOW IMAGINE THE OVAL IS A BALL WITH A CROSS ON IT...

YOU CAN MOVE THIS BALL TO MAKE THE FACE LOOK IN ANY DIRECTION!

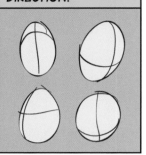

ONCE YOU GET THESE BASICS, YOU CAN VARY THE SHAPE OF THE BODY...

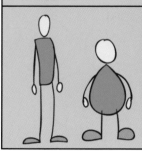

AND THE SHAPE OF THE HEAD.

OTHER OBJECTS ARE JUST AS EASY TO DRAW WITH A FEW BASIC SHAPES.

A PHONE IS JUST A FEW RECTANGLES...

AS IS A MONITOR, TABLE, OR CHAIR.

IT REALLY IS THAT EASY! JUST TRY IT OUT!

Whenever I explain what this book is about, I typically get the response, "That sounds really cool, but I can't draw." To which I explain that the method doesn't require any formal artistic training, save for a few pointers that I give.

Notice that I didn't use the word "artist," though. The reason for this is that I believe very much that everybody should consider himself or herself an artist, and I don't seem to be the only one.

In his book *Orbiting the Giant Hairball*, Gordon McKenzie gives an anecdote about how he visits various elementary schools to teach them about crafts. One of the first questions he asks each class is, "Who here is an artist?"

In the first grade, he would see a sea of hands raised and reaching for the sky. *Everybody* in first grade was an artist. By the second grade, the number of hands raised was halved, and by the third grade the number of hands was down to less than a handful of tentative hands.

What happened between the first and third grade? Was there an "artist exam" administered that informed the children whether they qualified as artists? Did somebody leave a memo to all the kids that informed them all to please put away their Crayolas unless they could make a half decent imitation of a human face? The answer, of course, is, "no."

Through some invisible societal pressures, the kids learned that the label of "artist" carried with it some minimum level of talent. In reality, I'd suggest that you're an artist whether you call yourself one or not. So long as you can draw a stick figure, you're well on your way to being able to create simple stories that explain your ideas better than any well-crafted words could.

I'm going to spend this chapter helping you feel comfortable drawing simple figures and expressions. If you feel pretty comfortable with your drawing skills already, then you should feel free to skim past this chapter.

Getting a Lot for a Little

In the last chapter, I talked about how abstracting away the details can actually be beneficial. The most abstract drawings are simple lines and shapes. A circle, and not necessarily a perfectly drawn circle, can depict many things. It can represent the sun, a head, a tire, or a ball, as shown in Figure 3.1. It all depends on where you put the circle. With just a few simple shapes, I think you can draw more than you realize.

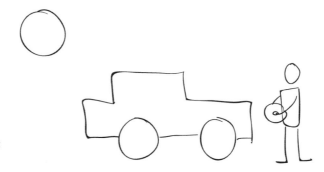

FIGURE 3.1
A circle can represent
many things.

For much of this book, I will be encouraging you to try sketching various
things as we progress. Of course, I can't actually see if you've got a pencil and
paper with you or not, but if you want to find out just how easy it is to create simple comics to communicate ideas, you definitely should get a pencil
for this chapter. Before we go further, I'll pause so you can go get yourself a
pencil (not so subtly shown in Figure 3.2). A pen will work just as well since
the things we're drawing are drawn so quickly that you can just redraw them
instead of erasing.

FIGURE 3.2
Get a pencil!

All right, now that you have the tools in hand (I'm trusting you here), let's
start with a few basic shapes. These will be your building blocks to draw
almost anything. Let's start with a circle, a straight-ish line, a curved line, a
rectangle, and a triangle. I say "straight-ish" because none of these shapes
need to be perfect. Nobody ever draws a perfect circle or a perfect straight
line. For the purposes of drawing these comics, yours don't need to be perfect either. I suspect your circle will look much like mine in Figure 3.3: more
like an oval and not meeting at the ends. That's perfectly fine!

FIGURE 3.3
Basic shapes: circle, lines, rectangle, and triangle.

With these basic shapes, and a few additional tricks, you'll be able to draw almost anything. To give an incredibly simple example, think about how a smiley face is constructed. There's a circle for the face, followed by two dots or lines for the eyes, a curve for the smile, and finally, if you're feeling fancy, two lines for eyebrows. When deconstructed this way, it seems a bit silly because the smiley face is already a fairly easy thing to draw, as shown in Figure 3.4. But anything that you think is hard to draw can actually be deconstructed in the same manner.

FIGURE 3.4
Deconstructing a smiley face.

People Are People

Now that we've deconstructed a smiley face, let's do the same for a basic figure. As you might suspect, there are a lot of different ways you can draw people, ranging from the classic stick figure to much more photo-realistic figures. With everything but the head, you can choose whether to draw the body part with a shape or a line.

For example, the body can be represented with a rectangle, a cone, or a rounder shape. The hands and feet can be represented as lines, or you can draw circles to give them more definition. What level of detail you choose to do is entirely up to you. I'm showing a number of different types in Figure 3.5, but let's use the simplest stick figures for a little bit and then I'll show how we can take that to make the more complex figures.

FIGURE 3.5
Some ways to draw a figure.

Proportions

When you draw a person, there are a few things to keep in mind in terms of proportions. Often, art books will suggest you use the size of the head as a way to measure the other proportions. This system is great for explaining the proportions, but in practice, you likely won't be measuring them exactly every time. Remember that this isn't a science, and you don't need to be exact to get your point across. As long as you get the proportions roughly correct and other people can recognize that you're drawing a person, you've accomplished your mission.

With that said, the proportions of a human body can be measured as two head heights for the chest, one head height for the hips and groin area, and three head heights for the legs. The elbows should come just below the waist and the knees halfway along the legs. I've drawn the proportions in dotted lines (each one represents the approximate height of the figure's head). Try it out! You can be exact with a ruler just to experiment, or you can try approximating the proportions. For now, feel free to just draw your figure standing straight facing you as I've shown in Figure 3.6.

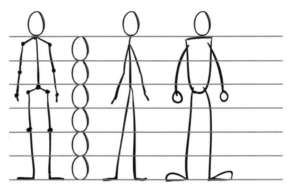

FIGURE 3.6
Proportions of a figure.

Body Language

Once you feel comfortable drawing a standing stick figure, we can start exploring the versatility of this simple construct. I mentioned earlier how comics, as a combination of words and pictures, can give more meaning to each area on its own. Depending on what action is taking place in the panel, the words can take on a completely different expressive meaning. In the example I gave, I used facial expressions to illustrate the idea, but it's equally powerful with just the body language.

You can tell a lot from the way a body is shaped. As you read the book right now, try adjusting your own body. If you lean your head down in front of you and hang your shoulders forward, how do you feel? How does that change if you hold your arms or put them in your pockets? Compare that feeling to raising your head above your spine and pushing your shoulders backward. Every day, we're subconsciously conveying and reading messages through body language. The direction you're leaning, where your hands are, how your feet are positioned, or even how far your head tilts all tell a story about how you're feeling.

In comics, we exaggerate expressions to get these messages across. It's remarkably easy to convey this body language with stick figures. Here are a few guidelines that will help you, with accompanying illustrations in Figure 3.7.

- **Leaning** forward can be used to show interest, concentration, or anger. The difference between interest and anger can depend on context but also on the arm position. Leaning backward can represent fear, apprehension, surprise, or rejection. Again, the difference between them is often just the context. You can also not lean at all, but curl the spine inward to show shyness or outward to show confidence.

- **Arm positions** can tell much of the story. If you are lifting a single arm overhead, you're representing anger or intimidation, while a hand on the chin indicates interest. Hands in front of the body may be guarding or fearful if leaning back, or anticipatory (like shaking a hand) if leaning forward. Scratching the head may represent puzzlement...but both hands up there may represent frustration! It's all about how you put these together.

- **Head positions** don't vary as much, but you can tell a lot both from the facial expression and where the person is looking. Whether the person is looking at the object or not indicates the level of interest or indifference. Even when indifferent, looking up and away is much more "I don't care," as opposed to looking down and away which suggests, "I'm shy or unsure."

FIGURE 3.7
Examples of body language.

One trick you can use to help figure out how a stick figure should look is imagining the emotion yourself. If you're angry, how do you act? What if you're *really* angry and yelling at somebody? Exaggerate the emotion and look at how your body reacts. I use this technique all the time. If you were sitting here watching me draw the examples in this chapter, you'd see me raising my arm, contorting my face, or scratching my head, trying to simulate whatever I'm drawing. Alternatively, take a picture of a friend in a pose, and then draw from that.

Drawing More Complex Figures

You don't have to draw anything more complex than stick figures to tell stories about people, but once you've mastered the stick figure poses, you'll be surprised how easy it is to do more. The stick figure drawing acts as a great foundation for the next step.

When most artists draw, whether they are drawing people or animals or cars, there is always a skeleton or guide that's drawn to help set proportions and perspective. These stick figures, much like the ones we just drew, define the shape and expression of the character. We can then add detail on top of the skeleton. Figure 3.8 shows two of the poses we drew earlier, with additional details added.

FIGURE 3.8
Adding definition to
the stick figure.

The level of detail you choose to add is up to you. Even creating blocks and cylinders out of the chest, hips, arms, and legs can make the character come alive. From there, you can take it one step further and add muscles and other details, as shown in Figure 3.9.

You can see how, no matter how complex the art, it always starts with the most basic components, with additional layers of complexity added one at a time.

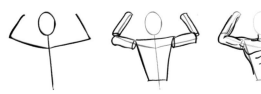

FIGURE 3.9
Adding meat to the
skeleton.

Faces

Psychologist Paul Ekman is known for his work in categorizing expressions—in particular, facial expressions. He created a system called the Facial Action Coding System (FACS) to categorize all the facial expressions possible. The manual is a 500-page tome. As expressive as body language is, it doesn't hold a candle to facial expressions. Luckily, drawing faces may be even easier than drawing stick figures.

Expressions

Drawing recognizable facial expressions isn't difficult. You only need to change two properties to create an enormous combination of expressions: the eyebrows and the mouth. Ekman's FACS has 46 base descriptors that are combined to categorize expressions. These descriptors include names such as "inner brow raiser," "lip corner puller," and "tongue show." Of the 46, 25 of them describe some action with the mouth and 11 of them describe an action with the eyes or eyebrows.

Not only are the expressions easy to create but they're also universally understood. In his studies, Ekman also found that many expressions, such as anger, joy, and sadness, are universally understood and didn't differ between cultures.

Let's start with a couple of basic expressions: joy and sadness. What's the difference between these expressions? The eyebrows are the same but the mouth has changed (see Figure 3.10). As the saying goes, "turn that frown upside down."

FIGURE 3.10
The two most basic faces.

Changing the mouth alone can create a dramatic difference in the emotion that's expressed. Let's explore what other ways we can draw the mouth. What if the mouth is flat? What does raising one side of the mouth higher than the other do to the expression? How about opening the mouth? Or showing the teeth? What changes occur if we stick out the tongue? None of these are hard to draw, and each one can change the emotion depicted, as shown in Figure 3.11.

FIGURE 3.11
Different mouth shapes.

Now try varying the eyebrows in a similar fashion. You can adjust the arches, make them flat, uneven, or furrowed (lots of eyebrow shapes in Figure 3.12).

FIGURE 3.12
Different eyebrow shapes.

Once again, the best way to understand what a face looks like for any given expression is to try it yourself. Look in a mirror and pretend to be happy, sad, angry, confused, shocked, or surprised. Exaggerate these expressions as much as possible and pay attention to your eyebrows and mouth. You're not going for the subtle acting that wins Academy Awards; you're aiming to make the expression as obvious to the reader as possible, and comics are excellent at exaggerations (see Figure 3.13).

FIGURE 3.13
Some other expressions: angry, confused, shocked, concentrating, and surprised.

Proportions

Let's do another quick exercise. Try to draw a face right now—not a smiley face, but a more realistic face with eyes, nose, and mouth. You can look at yourself in the mirror if you want. It doesn't need to be too detailed; your goal is just to have a face with all the features.

Now look at your sketch and look at where the eyes are relative to the top of the head. Are they a quarter of the way down? A third? What about the nose? Is that about halfway down? And the mouth?

For those who don't sketch often, it's common to draw a face with the nose around the center of the head and the eyes roughly a third of the way down from the top. In fact, for most faces, the eyes are in the middle.

If you draw an oval to represent a head, you can draw a cross to bisect the head in both directions. The horizontal line is where your eyes would be. If you split the bottom half into thirds, you'll roughly get the lines for the nose and the lips. That's all there is to drawing a face! Check out Figure 3.14.

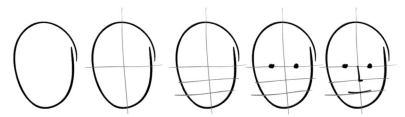

FIGURE 3.14
The proportions of a face.

This oval-and-cross method is how I start all of my drawings. Once you know how this works, you can draw heads and faces in any direction! Imagine the oval head as a three-dimensional ball and draw the cross over it in different ways, as shown in Figure 3.15. Even before you draw any of the facial features, you can already tell which way the face is facing!

FIGURE 3.15
Changing the direction of the face.

Settings and Objects

In many cases, you'll be using comics to tell the story of one or more people and how they relate to your product or service. Unless your service is another human, that means you'll need to draw the person interacting with some objects, as well as the environment.

As I said at the beginning of the chapter, drawing only requires the most basic shapes. I can't teach you to draw everything under the sun, but I can give you a few examples of common objects you might need to draw and how to deconstruct them to just a few basic shapes.

After you get the hang of drawing figures and faces, you can vary the shapes and sizes of them to create more variety. Everyone is built differently, so why not show it? If you keep the relative proportions in mind, it's pretty easy to stretch or squash a shape to create different body types.

Try drawing longer or shorter stick figures. Try using different shapes to represent the body—rounder shapes to add more body fat and more rectangular shapes to show more muscular builds, similar to Figure 3.16.

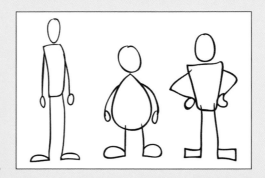

FIGURE 3.16
Different body shapes.

You can do the same with faces by adjusting the shape of the head. Try varying the shape of the oval or varying how rectangular the face is. You can also vary intersection points such as where the jawline meets the ears or the shape of the chin. And, of course, the shape of the facial features can be adjusted, too. Try changing the shape and size of the eyes, nose, and mouth (as shown in Figure 3.17).

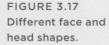

FIGURE 3.17
Different face and
head shapes.

Even the rules we learned earlier on where to position the facial features can be broken to exaggerate the character. Rules are made to be broken, but you have to know the rules before you can break them!

Look around you, and you'll start seeing faces in a completely different way. I take the bus to work every day, and I sometimes find myself looking at people and observing the shapes of their heads, noses, lips, and more. It really changes what "people watching" means when you start paying attention to the details of how people lean, how they hold their book, or how they stand.

If you're reading this book, there's a good chance what you're building or designing involves computers or phones. Let's look at how you might draw a person at a computer or using a phone, similar to Figure 3.18.

FIGURE 3.18
Almost anything can be represented with basic shapes.

See how simple the shapes can be? Most objects can be represented with a few well-placed rectangles! It's all about where you see the rectangle that informs the reader of what it is. The "phone" I drew is nothing more than a rectangle, yet its size and the way it is held gives enough indication of what it is.

Sometimes, you'll want to show part of the screen itself, as shown in Figure 3.19. While it's tempting to just take up the entire panel to show the screen, it's also possible to still show part of the person using the computer or phone to keep the panel interesting.

FIGURE 3.19
You can still show the person when looking at a screen.

In addition to the objects your character interacts with, there's also the background to consider. Backgrounds help set the context for the story, telling the reader where the character is. They can also act as a point of reference. I might draw a door in the background and, through subsequent panels, change the position of the door to show that the character is walking (see Figure 3.20).

FIGURE 3.20
Using the background to show movement.

But that level of detail is rarely necessary if you're just trying to get an idea across. Quite often, you don't need to draw any background at all. It can make the comic look fuller, but remember your goal: to quickly communicate an idea. You should only draw backgrounds if you feel you need to set context.

For example, maybe it's important to show that your character is shopping, and to indicate that, you draw the character walking past a storefront. Or perhaps it's important to show the character is outdoors, say, in a park. Whatever the reason, if you do feel you need to draw backgrounds, don't fret too much over the details. Just make sure to get enough detail for the reader to recognize the scene. One trick you can use to help differentiate the background from the foreground is to use a thinner pen so that the foreground stands out, as shown in Figure 3.21.

FIGURE 3.21
Differentiating the background with line thickness.

How to Show Action in Your Cartoons

How to Draw It (http://howtodrawit.com) *is a fantastic website containing many tutorials on how to draw cartoons and animals. It's published and maintained in Santa Fe, New Mexico, by Pam Neely. This is one of her tutorials about showing action. I recommend you check out her entire series on cartooning on her site.*

Get ready for good long periods of wilting fatigue, muscular exhilaration, heart-throbbing suspense, agonized tension, aching jaws, and stiff, seemingly immovable joints. Because, when you draw human figures in any action, physical or mental, you are bound to feel the action intensely.

You cannot draw without feeling. And the more strongly you feel, the better cartoonist you are sure to be, provided you can effectively transfer your feeling to paper.

Draw a man running like mad, fist clenched, jaw set. What happens to you? Try it. Put yourself wholeheartedly and deeply into the action you are drawing, and I guarantee you will feel it. You will be exhausted when you finish drawing a man running hard—if you put yourself into it. But when you finally do produce a drawing that is really convincing, it compensates you for the pain you felt when you were drawing.

Never draw any action without taking the pose yourself. Even if you have a model to pose for you, you must get the feel of it first yourself. Whether you look at yourself in a mirror or not does not matter. You will unconsciously draw convincingly if you are thinking how it feels while you draw.

Use the stick figure or any other rough-in method you like and draw as many action figures as you can. Learn to exaggerate the action much more than would normally be probable in any figure. This is another secret of good cartooning (Figure 3.22).

FIGURE 3.22
Exaggerate the action.

Summary

We've come a long way in just a few pages—from circles and rectangles to human figures and facial expressions. Here are some things to keep in mind as you draw:

- Everything is composed of simple, basic shapes such as circles, triangles, and lines.

- Focus on the eyebrows and mouth to make a face expressive.

- You can measure a body proportions as "heads." The chest is the height of two heads, the hip another, and the legs three more.

- Which way the body leans or poses can communicate as much expression as whether the face is smiling or not.

- Once you have the basic skeleton down, you can add more complexity as you please.

Even if you haven't been drawing along through the chapter (I know, that pencil is so far away), I hope you feel pretty confident that you can at least draw a stick figure and smiley face that represent the emotion and action you want to convey.

CHAPTER 4

What's Your Comic About?

LET'S TALK ABOUT HOW TO CREATE A COMIC.

WE'LL SPEND A CHAPTER ON EACH OF THE FOUR STEPS IN THE PROCESS.

FIRST, YOU HAVE TO ANSWER. "WHAT'S YOUR COMIC ABOUT?" THAT'S THIS CHAPTER.

THEN, YOU WRITE THE STORY IN SCRIPT FORM, LIKE A MOVIE.

OUTDOORS

Joe is running

JANE

Where are you

OE

LAYING OUT THE COMIC COMES NEXT.

AND FINALLY, YOU DRAW AND REFINE THE COMIC.

IN THE TEXT VERSION, I'LL ALSO GO THROUGH THE PROCESS WITH AN EXAMPLE: CREATING A COMIC FOR A PRODUCT CALLED *SQUARE*.

PAY

SO LET'S TALK ABOUT THE FIRST STEP: WHAT'S YOUR COMIC ABOUT?

TO ANSWER, YOU FIRST HAVE TO LOOK AT A FEW FACTORS.

GOALS OF YOUR COMIC: IS YOUR COMIC TRYING TO EXPLAIN A CONCEPT?

OR TO DRIVE MORE SALES?

BUY!

LENGTH OF COMIC

I RECOMMEND COMICS THAT ARE 3-8 PANELS LONG.

PEOPLE ARE MORE LIKELY TO READ IT.

LONGER COMICS MIGHT BE APPROPRIATE IF YOU COULD ACTUALLY HAND IT OUT IN PHYSICAL FORM.

THE AUDIENCE FOR YOUR COMIC: KNOWING WHO YOUR AUDIENCE IS CHANGES HOW YOU WRITE THE COMIC.

THEY MIGHT BE EXPERTS...

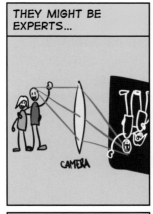

...OR NOT.

AND THEIR CONTEXT MATTERS.

WHERE ARE YOU?

AT HOME.

IN SAN FRANCISCO.

IN MY CAR.

A REPRESENTATIVE USE CASE: LASTLY, TELL A STORY THAT HIGHLIGHTS THE RIGHT FEATURES, AND SPEAKS TO A USER'S PROBLEM.

ABC   ABC

FOR EXAMPLE, APPLE'S FACETIME VIDEOCONFERENCING WASN'T EXPLAINED IN TERMS OF FEATURES.

BLAH BLAH GAJILLION PIXELS...

BUT INSTEAD, THROUGH RELATABLE LIFE STORIES.

HI DADDY!

When you create a product or feature, there's a product development process you undergo. For example, you might start by interviewing some existing customers or running some focus groups. You might create business and functional requirements describing what you need. Then, when you're ready, you begin design and development and iterate on the product. Or perhaps you prefer to define products by first building a prototype, bypassing formal requirements. Everyone has his or her own preferred process. What process you use and how strictly you follow it depends on circumstances.

The Comic Creation Process

The same can be said for creating a comic: there isn't one correct way to go about it. I'll present a comic creation process that includes all the steps involved in creating a comic, but it's just one of many approaches. The more practiced you are at it, the better you will be at knowing which steps you need to spend the most time on and which steps you can combine or skip over entirely.

The process of creating a comic for your product can be broken down into the following steps. For larger projects, you might feel the need to create multiple comics that represent different personas and use cases. In the case of the comics we created for Yahoo!, we created a total of three comics. Each comic represented very different use cases that resonated with different participants. The goal was to be representative, not comprehensive.

1. **What's your comic about?**

    Before creating the comic, you need to decide why you're using comics and what to include in the story. What features do you want to highlight, or more importantly, which features can be excluded from the story? Who is the product for and who will be reading the comic? The output from this step should be a few bullet points of things you want to highlight. If you were planning a presentation or essay, this is the equivalent of setting up the thesis and main talking points. This step is what we'll talk about in detail in this chapter.

2. **Writing the story.**

    Once you've decided which aspects you're going to highlight in the comic, the next step is to create a script. Just as a movie starts from the scripting phase, we'll define the comic in words first before drawing the comic. The purpose of this step is to define what the progression of the story is. If the first step were defining a thesis, then this step would be defining the outline. You'll define the characters that are in the comic, the settings where the story is told, and the dialogue that will be spoken either by narration or by the characters.

3. **Laying out the comic.**

   Even when the story has been defined, there are still a lot of decisions that need to be made about the composition of a comic. Just as photographers, filmmakers, or painters must decide what parts of a scene they want to capture, each panel in a comic has to be carefully planned. Do you want to show the building they're in? Do you choose to show a close-up of the product? How much, if any, of the interface should you show? I've talked about how comics are very powerful for representing movement and time. If comics are sequential art, then part of the process is deciding how to sequence the story in such a way that your readers can follow it.

4. **Drawing and refining the comic.**

   Once you have the basic sequencing and layout prepared, you can put in the finishing touches to the comic (see Figure 4.1). I'll cover some additional tips and tricks to augment the basic drawing techniques covered in Chapter 3, "You Don't Need to Be an Artist." A lot of tools also exist to make comic creation easier. I'll share a range of resources, including drawing software and layout templates, to make the process of creating comics even faster.

FIGURE 4.1
The comic creation process.

To help illustrate each of these steps more clearly, I'll use an example and create a comic from start to finish over the next four chapters. The example is a real product, but to my knowledge, they haven't used comics in their product development or marketing . So let's pretend we've been asked to create a comic for them.

The Example: Square

Square is a little physical card reader which you can plug into the headphone jack of an Android phone, an iPhone, or an iPad (see Figure 4.2). After you plug it in, you can accept payments from any major credit card with minimal initial setup. It's currently used by small businesses, coffee shops, street food carts, people who are selling items on Craigslist, garage sales, and many others. This card reading device and its associated software are free, but each time you run a transaction, a flat rate is charged to the merchant.

FIGURE 4.2
The Square credit card reader.

I feel that Square is a very appropriate example for a number of reasons. First, it's a product that spans many devices, including mobile devices, tablet devices, and a website. Second, the product has many use cases and personas, which is probably the case for many of your products. Finally, there are clear, real-world interactions that can be associated with the story of Square's usage.

If you'd like more information on Square, you can look up the product at http://squareup.com. It's worth mentioning that the founder of Square is also a co-founder at Twitter, where I used to work. However, my use of their product as this book's example is without any consultation or inside knowledge of their product. We'll go into more detail with this example soon and continue doing so for the next few chapters.

Now that we have an example to work with, let's start the first step of the comic creation process by answering the question: What's your comic about? Take a look at Figure 4.3.

FIGURE 4.3
What's your comic about?

Answering this question can be tricky. Instead of approaching it as one broad and vague question, it might be easier to break it down into a few logical steps. Once you have addressed these, it should be much easier to narrow down your comic story.

1. **Define the goals of your comic.** What do you want to get out of it? What is the next step you want the reader to take after reading your comic?

2. **Decide on the length of your comic.** The length will dictate how much detail you give and how precise your messaging needs to be.

3. **Identify the audience for your comic.** Your story may change, depending on the audience's expertise level and the context in which you're portraying your comic.

4. **Select a representative use case.** Think of a scenario that shows off your product well. Once you find that, the scenario will naturally help you narrow down which features to highlight.

Goals of Your Comic

Before thinking about what's in the comic, you should start with what you want the comic to accomplish. If you know what actions you hope to inspire through the comic, then you can design the comic toward that goal. When Google decided to create their comic for Google Chrome, they had a clear goal in mind. They didn't want people to focus on feature comparisons between browsers; instead, they wanted readers to gain an understanding of their technical motivations for building a Web browser from scratch.

The goal of the comic may vary, depending on whether it's for a product that exists or not. When using comics to describe products that haven't been built, the goals may be centered on understanding and sponsorship. The comics we created at Yahoo! were to validate our product vision with potential users as well as management. Our goal was to get feedback on how useful the product ideas were and to get support from management to start building the product as described in the comic.

Sometimes, the goal can be completely measurable. At Raptr, we used a comic on the homepage to describe the product. Our goal was to help visitors understand our product, but there was a specific action we were also hoping to inspire—user sign-ups. Similarly, since Square is a product that's already in the market, the goal of our fictitious comic should be to help merchants understand why it's useful and ultimately to have them sign up to receive a Square device. Defining the goal of your comic is a crucial step, but it shouldn't be that difficult. If you've already decided to create a comic, chances are you have some idea what you're hoping to accomplish from it.

The Length of Your Comic

After deciding what your comic is about, the next important factor is to determine how long your comic will be, because you need to know how much room you have to work with. I encourage the use of very short comics (3–8 panels) to illustrate an idea. At that length, they're easy to consume, yet they contain enough information both for internal and external communication. The comic should fit on the homepage of a site, on a postcard, or in an email to your team. However, there are plenty of examples of longer form comics.

The Google Chrome comic, mentioned in a sidebar in Chapter 2, "Properties of Comics," was over 30 pages and was fairly technical in nature (see Figure 4.4). Even at that length, it was much more digestible than a detailed white paper and represented just the right balance for readability. The comic was available online, but it was also distributed in physical form to key developers and industry experts.

The U.S. Navy, as a way to connect to its Japanese audience, created a full *Manga* (Japanese form of comics) book in both English and Japanese to explain why their aircraft carrier would need to be docked in Japan for several months (see Figure 4.5). Given the widespread acceptance of *Manga* as a medium for any topic, this seems like a great way to connect with their audience. A lot of people were interested in the carrier so publicizing the comic wasn't difficult. Many local and online press outlets wrote articles about the comic. When they released the book, there was a line around the block to get a copy of the book!

FIGURE 4.4
A copy of the Google Chrome comic book.

FIGURE 4.5
Manga for U.S. Navy's USS Washington.

Another example of longer form comics in use comes from Adobe's Evangeline Haughey, who was trying to find creative ways to encourage team members to read her user research reports and decided to spice one of her reports up by presenting it in comic book form. It was a handful of pages, and she printed them as booklets, complete with a fake comic book cover illustrated by her colleague Julie Meridian (see Figure 4.6).

FIGURE 4.6
Adobe's comic book cover.

One commonality between these examples of longer form comics is that they all feature a physical component to their distribution. If your ideas are more complex or lengthy, consider creating longer comics but also think about ways to distribute physical copies of the comic. It's surprising how hard it is *not* to read a copy of a comic that's in your hand!

Longer form comics aren't always appropriate, however. Akoha, a start-up that uses trading cards to encourage "doing good deeds," tried to use comics to explain their services in an innovative fashion. Unfortunately, it was a multi-page comic that few visited when coming to their homepage. In contrast, many companies, such as Nectar, used very simple three-panel comics on their homepage (see Figure 4.7). These comics were easy to consume and immediately explained the product.

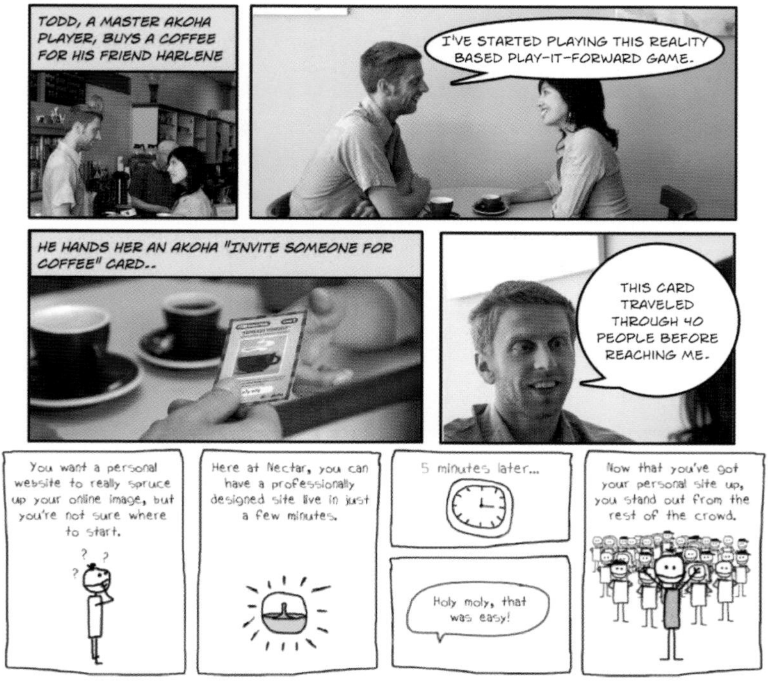
TODD, A MASTER AKOHA PLAYER, BUYS A COFFEE FOR HIS FRIEND HARLENE
I'VE STARTED PLAYING THIS REALITY BASED PLAY-IT-FORWARD GAME.
HE HANDS HER AN AKOHA "INVITE SOMEONE FOR COFFEE" CARD..
THIS CARD TRAVELED THROUGH 40 PEOPLE BEFORE REACHING ME.
You want a personal website to really spruce up your online image, but you're not sure where to start.
Here at Nectar, you can have a professionally designed site live in just a few minutes.
5 minutes later...
Holy moly, that was easy!
Now that you've got your personal site up, you stand out from the rest of the crowd.

FIGURE 4.7
Akoha's multi-page comic vs. Nectar's three-panel comic.

I love constraints. We've all seen the power of using them. Presentations are constrained by time and reports by number of pages. In movies, the editing process is crucial to ensure that the film is under a certain number of minutes. This process culls the unnecessary scenes that do not add to the depth of the story. These constraints may seem artificial, but you'll find that they're helpful, forcing you to be creative and thoughtful. By constraining a comic from three to eight panels, you're forced to think about what features are most important to convey.

How Common Craft Distills Ideas into Simple Animated Videos

*Lee LeFever cofounded Common Craft (*http://commoncraft.com*) with his wife Sachi. They make explanatory videos that are short and simple, made out of paper cutouts and a whiteboard (like in Figure 4.8). They have become experts in explaining complex subjects, and Lee's upcoming book,* The Art of Explanation, *will help professionals improve their explanation skills. Common Craft has built a library of videos for educators and worked with companies like Intel, Google, Ford Motors, and Dropbox. In total, their videos have been viewed over 50 million times. I sat with Lee for a few minutes at the South by Southwest Interactive festival and asked him about his approach.*

FIGURE 4.8
Common Craft characters are simple figures.

How did you come up with the idea for this format?

Starting in school and going into my work in the tech industry, I always felt that good, easy-to-understand explanations were in short supply. The geeks were doing the explaining and doing it poorly. We started making videos to solve this problem. In terms of the visual format, it was Sachi's (my wife and partner) idea. I tried standing in front of a whiteboard and talking to the camera to explain an idea, and it was, let's say, discouraging. She saw the potential to point the camera down onto the whiteboard and use paper cut-outs, markers, and hands. The format has been consistent since the first video and is now being adopted by teachers who build simple videos with students and call them "Common Craft Style" videos. We love to be an inspiration for educators.

Can you walk me through what the process is for creating a video? How long does it take?

We approach all our videos with the same goal: to make an idea easier to understand in three minutes. Over the years, we've come to a number of conclusions about how to make this happen. From our perspective, great explanations are based on empathy and confidence. In order to make an idea easy to understand, you must put yourself in the audience's shoes and *empathize* with their perspective, knowledge, ideas. Then, you think about your communication in terms of building and sustaining the audience's *confidence*. This means starting with context and the basic ideas before moving into details. We always say—forest first, then the trees.

In terms of production, every video is different, but they usually follow a similar process. We give Common Craft members the ability to suggest and vote on potential titles. This is a big help in knowing what videos to make. Once we decide on a title, we do research and talk a lot about the big ideas, what the audience needs, and how we can approach it. This can take hours or weeks, depending on a number of factors like our existing knowledge of the subject. Next we write the script, which is the heart of our work—where the explanation truly resides. This process is very iterative and represents the biggest chunk of time. Once we feel good about the script, we create and iterate on the storyboard and shoot the video. Shooting is usually done over two days and takes around six hours—all live-action stop-motion. Then post-production begins and can take 8–12 hours. All told, I'd say a video takes around 40–50 hours to create.

The Audience for Your Comic

Aside from comic length, the Google Chrome and U.S. Navy comics also share something else in common. Both comics had a very clear understanding of who their audience was and had stories specifically tailored for them. In the case of Google Chrome, the audience was technical enough to care about browser performance and engineering. With that in mind, they were able to tell stories about JavaScript processing and browser caching. For the U.S. Navy, an understanding of their audience—Japanese residents of Yokosuka—determined the format of their messaging. In fact, they were so successful in that campaign, people lined up around the street to get a copy of the printed *Manga*.

Who your audience is, where they're from, and what they know can influence the contents and delivery of your story. Let's say somebody asked you, "How do I get to the nearest post office?" What would you say? Maybe something like:

> Turn left at the first light, keep going until the stop sign, and then make a right on Main street.

These directions seem pretty straightforward, but what if you knew the person asking you? Let's say, it's your cousin Joseph who's a bit navigationally challenged. Then you could give a few more details.

> Turn left at the first light where the blue gas station is. Keep going—you'll pass that playground we used to play at—and make a right when you see our old high school.

What you're doing is offering the right level of detail based on the person you are communicating the information to. We actually scope our conversations based on context and audience all the time without even realizing it. If you had answered the question with every painstaking detail, it would be more like this:

> Insert your key into the ignition; turn it once until you feel the engine starting. Before you back out of your garage, make sure to check all your mirrors for any people or vehicles...

...and so on. We don't go into this level of detail because we implicitly understand and consider the audience's expertise level. This is an important consideration but insufficient. Beyond the expertise level, we also want to consider the audience's context. In the previous example, I assumed that the person was asking for driving directions and was a driver. However, the person asking for directions might be a bicyclist or pedestrian. To a bicyclist, the grade of the street is important; a pedestrian doesn't cares about one-way streets; and drivers can't drive down stairs.

Now let's look at a business context. In *Design of Everyday Things*, Don Norman discusses the concept of mental models—how people view a system. Norman uses a camera as an example. If you were to ask an engineer how a camera works, you might get an explanation about light, aperture, and shutter speed. The comic for such an explanation might look like Figure 4.9.

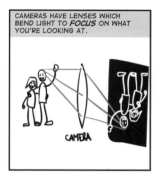

FIGURE 4.9
How a camera works.

However, if you were to ask a layperson how a camera works, they might tell you about how to turn it on, how to focus, and how to upload a picture. Then the comic might look like Figure 4.10.

FIGURE 4.10
How a camera works to a layperson.

Both of these comics are correct. They simply differ based on the expertise of the audience and the context of what the audience is hoping to learn from the story. If you know your audience, you'll have a much better idea of what your story is and how to frame it. We can apply these considerations to our Square example, too. For Square, our audience is potential merchants who have trouble receiving credit card payments and might find Square useful. These merchants need to be smartphone owners, so they are presumably reasonably tech-savvy. At the same time, they only care that the device is easy to use and secure, but are unlikely to understand (or care) about the detailed technical workings of the hardware.

Selecting a Representative Use Case

You now know whom you want to read your comic and its context. The next step is to find a story that helps your readers understand why they should care! To accomplish that, you need to find a use case that resonates with them and their problems. Sometimes, you're trying to tell a story of a problem they didn't even realize they had.

When Apple launched its iPhone 4 and videoconferencing application, Face-Time, we already had many competitive and compelling products we could use. Skype, Google Talk, and even Apple's own iChat had free video chat and even video conferencing capabilities. One important distinction was that it was on the phone rather than on a computer—but given you had to still be connected to a WiFi network, this portability was limited.

Apple didn't explain FaceTime's differentiation through a list of features. Instead, they aired a series of short and powerful advertisements that showcased powerful, human use cases—scenarios such as a father traveling abroad and conferencing in with his family, or grandparents seeing their grandchild for the first time (see Figure 4.11). Are these scenarios unique to FaceTime? Certainly not, but they were compelling and helped the viewer relate to why the feature was important to them.

Now let's go back to Square. What kind of use cases could we use for Square? Let's list a few situations where we think Square would most help solve a problem.

- Trade shows
- Selling large items on craigslist
- Coffee shops
- Garage sales

- Small merchants
- Food stands
- Massage therapist
- Musicians

FIGURE 4.11
Apple's FaceTime advertisement.

Notice the overall theme of the use cases listed here. In each case, the users do not typically have an easy means of accepting credit card payments but find themselves in situations where they need to do so or lose business. For some, such as coffee shops and small merchants, the users have an established business. Other use cases are around individuals who may need to accept credit cards on occasions when they're running garage sales or selling items on craigslist. Others still may be in the goods and services business, providing their services in various locations including conferences, craft fairs, or people's homes. Two themes arise from looking at these use cases: there's the advantage of Square's mobility and the advantage of Square's ease of access to a credit card payment system.

Conceivably, we could create just one comic on the mobile use case, and it would inherently also describe the easy credit card payment system. However, if we were actually creating these for Square, it would probably be beneficial to have a separate comic for merchants lest they think, "Well, that's nice, but my shop doesn't move around so I don't need a mobile solution." For the purposes of this book's example, let's take the use case of selling books at tradeshows and conferences and create a comic around that. For that use case, which of Square's features should we highlight? Maybe it will be useful to list all the features:

- Free App on iPhone, iPad, and Android.

- Free card reader device that plugs into the mobile device's headphones jack.

- Accepts Visa, Mastercard, American Express, and Discover.

- Purchasers can use their fingers or a stylus to sign their signatures on the phone or iPad.

- If the card can't be read, there's an option to enter the number manually.

- A lot of focus is placed on the design of the card reader, the website, and the mobile applications.

- Money received is deposited daily to your bank account.

- A flat fee of 2.75% is charged for all transactions.

- The purchaser can get a receipt by email or text message.

- The vendor does not have to commit to any contract to receive the device or use the service.

- From the website, the vendor can track a history of all invoices.

- All transactions are secure.

- Full reports on what was sold.

- Regular customers can set up a tab.

Yikes! That's a lot of features to include in a story. How are we going to create a comic with only 3–8 panels that encompass all of these points? There are more bullet points than panels! Luckily, we have a use case now to help us narrow down which features are important to highlight and which are less so. Important aspects include the fact that it's a device that plugs into popular mobile devices and accepts all major credit cards. It's debatable whether the cost of the device (free) is something that you need to highlight in the comic. You could argue that the comic gets the reader interested enough to investigate, and you could subsequently explain the details. However, as you'll find later, it's easy enough to incorporate the cost into the dialogue.

Some details that you can skip in the comic include how often the money received is deposited, the fees, and the lack of a contract. All of these elements are important selling points for the product, but remember the questions the comic should answer: "What is this and why should I care?" Can you imagine if the iPhone 4 commercials talked about their two-year contracts or even the cost of the phone?

Summing up, here are the features that seem most important to highlight for the mobile payment use case we're doing:

- Free App on iPhone, iPad, and Android.

- Free card reader device that plugs into the mobile device's headphones jack.

- Card reader accepts Visa, Mastercard, American Express, and Discover.

- Purchasers can use their fingers or a stylus to sign their signatures on the phone or iPad.

- The purchaser can get a receipt by email or text message.

- From the website, the vendor can track a history of all invoices.

That list seems much more manageable. Can you see the story crystallizing? You've decided the goal of the comic is to get merchants to understand Square and sign up for one. The audience for the comic is merchants who are technologically savvy. The problem you're going to showcase is someone selling goods at tradeshows and conferences with no easy way to accept credit cards. In particular, you'll create a story around a person who wants to sell books at a conference. (As it turns out, Lou Rosenfeld and Rosenfeld Media, the publisher of this very book, now use Square to sell their books at conferences!) Finally, you have narrowed down the feature list to just over a handful to highlight. Now that you know what the story is about, let's talk about how to write it!

Brad Colbow is a Web designer, illustrator, and cartoonist. He is the creator of The Brads, *a Web comic on technology and design. He also creates informational comics on various subjects, such as HTML5 with Jeremy Keith and Mental Models with Indi Young. Brad explains how he goes about taking a subject and breaking it down into a comic.*

Most of my information comics tackle technical subjects. A long detailed article or blog post is a great way to share knowledge, but sometimes a brief overview can be valuable—that's where a comic shines.

1. **Understand the subject.** I try to gather as many sources I can on a topic to see how different people approach it. I take notes and start to figure out what information is important and what I can leave out.

2. **Break it down to its most basic parts.** I start with a simple outline, a bulleted list of the most important information, or sketch out some notes. For example, if I'm writing about touch gestures for the iPhone, I might list dozens of them, but for a comic I probably just want to focus on a handful (see Figure 4.12).

    To narrow it down, I might take a look at the most popular apps and see what they use or just summarize what a touch gesture is (Figure 4.13).

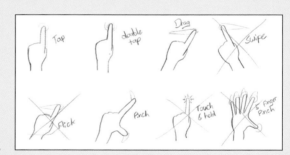

FIGURE 4.12
A visual bullet list of important information.

FIGURE 4.13
Summarizing touch gestures.

Often at this stage I'll reach out to someone who's very knowledgeable on the topic and share what I'm working on to make sure I'm on the right track and not missing anything important.

3. **Fleshing it out.** Now it starts to look like a comic. I start to figure out how many panels there will be and what information goes in what panel. Since the topics are dense, I try not to put too much text in any one panel.

4. **Come up with a theme.** If you just have a narrator speaking, you wouldn't have much of a comic. In "Misunderstanding Markup," I had the narrator (writer Jeremy Keith) coming back from a shopping trip. The food made a nice metaphor to visually play off when drawing (Figure 4.14).

FIGURE 4.14
Using grocery items as a theme for the comic.

5. **Illustrating.** Once all the content is in place and makes sense, I can move forward with the fun part, drawing.

Summary

In this chapter, I introduced you to the four steps of creating a comic: deciding what your comic is about, writing the story, laying out the comic, and then drawing the comic. We started on our example comic for the mobile payments start-up, Square, and will continue to build the comic through the next few chapters.

The first step in creating a comic is deciding what you want the comic to be about. You can break down that question into four components to be answered separately:

1. Define the goals of your comic.

2. Decide on the length of your comic.

3. Identify the audience for your comic.

4. Select a representative use case.

Once you've determined the answer to each of these components, you can then start scripting the comic and creating the story!

CHAPTER 5

Writing the Story

COMICS START AS THEY DO IN MOVIES—WITH A WRITTEN SCRIPT.

YOU DON'T HAVE TO USE THE SAME CONVENTION, BUT WHY RE-INVENT THE WHEEL?

SCENE: Interior of conference center. SETTING
NICOLE CHARACTER
Do you take credit card?
LOU ⌐DIALOGUE
Sure! Any card you like.
LOU swipes Nicole's card through the Square reader
⌐ACTION

THE ***SETTING*** IS THE CONTEXT WHERE THE ACTION IS TAKING PLACE.

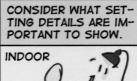

I'M IN A CAR.

I'M ON MY WAY.

I'M IN HONG KONG, MEETING A CLIENT.

CONSIDER WHAT SETTING DETAILS ARE IMPORTANT TO SHOW.

INDOOR

OUTDOOR

AT HOME

AT WORK

NIGHT TIME

DAY TIME

THE **CHARACTERS** IN YOUR COMIC SHOULD BE BASED ON EXISTING OR INTENDED USERS OF YOUR PRODUCT.

Mark
Age: 35-45
Industry:
Internet

Likes independent bands and flannel. Has a tendency to

YOU SHOULD KNOW WHO THESE PEOPLE ARE FROM INTERVIEWS OR OTHER RESEARCH.

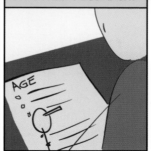

THE **DIALOGUE** OF YOUR CHARACTERS IS A CRUCIAL ELEMENT IN YOUR COMIC.

WHAT THEY SAY NEEDS TO BE REALISTIC.

THERE IS SO MUCH TO DO IN DOWNIEVILLE THAT I WILL HAVE TO CREATE A COLLECTION OF POINTS!

TRY TO AVOID "GEE WHIZ!" DIALOGUE AND STAY TRUE TO THE CHARACTERS.

THERE'S SO MUCH TO DO! HOW AM I GOING TO KEEP TRACK?!

HOW THE DIALOGUE IS DISPLAYED MATTERS, TOO. FROM THE STYLE OF THE TYPE...

TO THE STYLE OF THE SPEECH BUBBLES.

ONE OTHER THING TO WATCH OUT FOR IS THE OVERUSE OF CAPTIONS.

TRY TO USE DIALOGUE TO TELL THE STORY...

KEVIN WENT HOME, HAD A CUP OF COFFEE, AND WALKED 20 MINS BACK HERE TO SAY...

...INSTEAD OF THE CAPTIONS FILLING IN TOO MUCH.

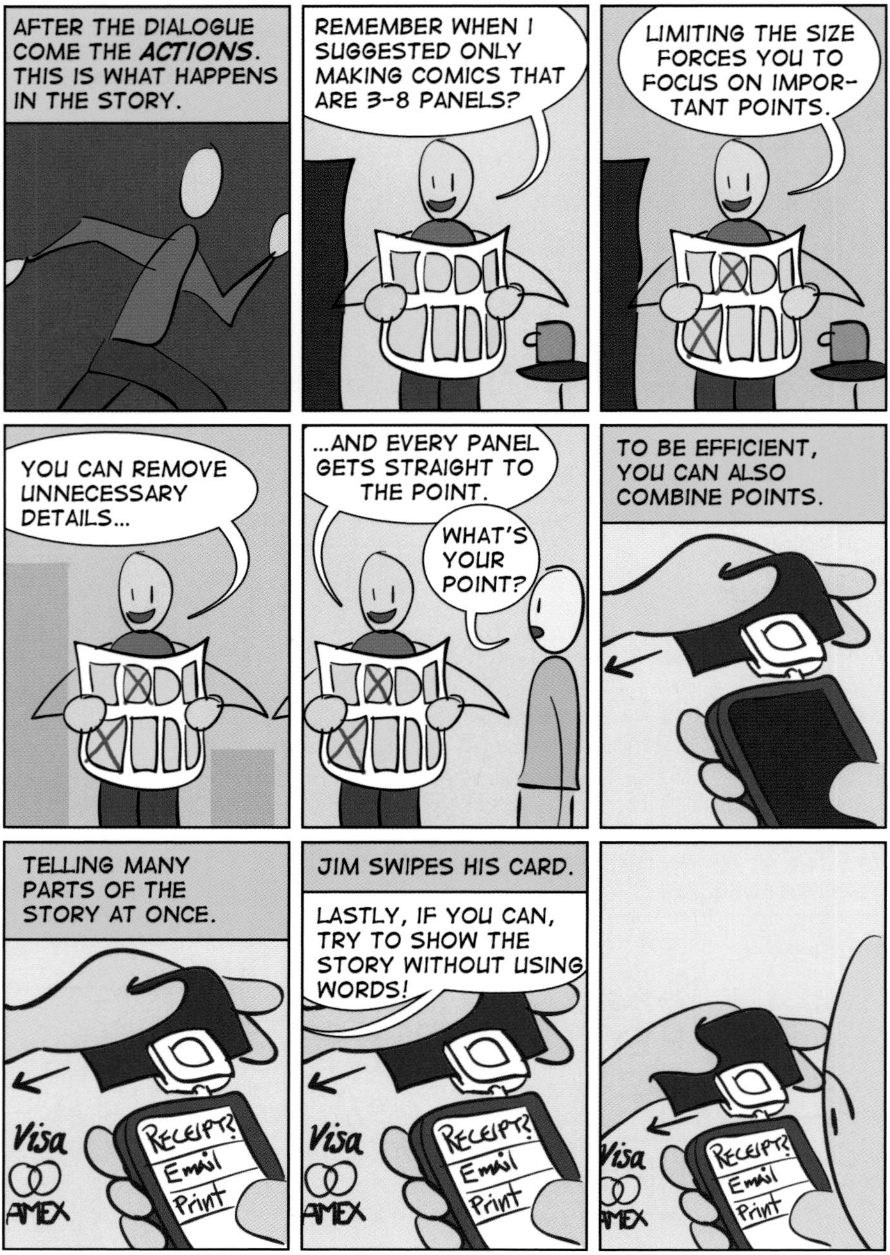
AFTER THE DIALOGUE COME THE *ACTIONS*. THIS IS WHAT HAPPENS IN THE STORY.
REMEMBER WHEN I SUGGESTED ONLY MAKING COMICS THAT ARE 3-8 PANELS?
LIMITING THE SIZE FORCES YOU TO FOCUS ON IMPOR-TANT POINTS.
YOU CAN REMOVE UNNECESSARY DETAILS...
...AND EVERY PANEL GETS STRAIGHT TO THE POINT.
WHAT'S YOUR POINT?
TO BE EFFICIENT, YOU CAN ALSO COMBINE POINTS.
TELLING MANY PARTS OF THE STORY AT ONCE.
Visa
AMEX
RECEIPT?
Email
Print
JIM SWIPES HIS CARD.
LASTLY, IF YOU CAN, TRY TO SHOW THE STORY WITHOUT USING WORDS!
Visa
AMEX
RECEIPT?
Email
Print
Visa
AMEX
RECEIPT?
Email
Print

After deciding what your comic is about, the second step in the comic creation process is to write out the story (see Figure 5.1). This part of the process still doesn't involve much, if any, drawing. The focus is on telling the story, with an understanding that it will eventually be told in comic form.

FIGURE 5.1
Writing the story.

Effective storytelling, whether in prose, movies, or comics, is a skill of its own. There are many resources on the topic. Whitney Quesenbery's and Kevin Brook's book *Storytelling for User Experience* may be a good companion resource to read. Within this chapter, we'll focus on how to plan and document a story to make it easier to draw the comic later.

At eBay, designers Shailesh Shilwant and Deb Aoki use comics and drawing extensively to communicate their ideas. They liken the technique to watching a movie:

> "When you are watching a movie, you hopefully watch it all at once. When you're making a movie, you never see it all at once. You're making it in 15 different parts."
>
> —Shailesh

> "When you have a full storyboard, you can see the full story arc so you can see where it's really slow or where you can cut out a scene instead of focusing on specific areas like how big to make an explosion."
>
> —Deb

Instead of focusing on the minutiae of specific features, you can use comics to help people see the whole story in one arc up front. So how do you write that story down? How do you describe a comic in words?

A Crash Course in Scriptwriting

The movie analogy that Shailesh and Deb used to describe comics is actually incredibly apt. Much like movies, many comic writers also write out their story beforehand by using similar scripting conventions comparable to movie scriptwriters. For example, let's take a look at the script for *Romeo and Juliet* from the most celebrated scriptwriter, William Shakespeare.

SCENE: A churchyard; in it a tomb belonging to the Capulets.

PARIS

I do defy thy conjurations,

And apprehend thee for a felon here.

ROMEO

Wilt thou provoke me? Then have at thee, boy!

They fight

PAGE

O Lord, they fight! I will go call the watch.

Exit

PARIS

O, I am slain!

Falls

If thou be merciful,

Open the tomb, lay me with Juliet.

Dies

The script is composed of four primary elements, which are specially formatted:

- **Setting** of the scene is defined up front, often in bold. It describes the time of day, the location, whether it's indoors or outdoors, and if necessary, even the city or country. The setting may also include what's going on in the background.

- **Characters** are usually defined in all caps and bolded. They're also used as titles to indicate who is speaking.

- **Dialogue** is what is being spoken, and it follows the character. Dialogue is typically printed in regular type.

- **Actions**, often taken by the characters, are usually in italics.

While not all writers use this convention for comics, it is one that suits our needs very well. Each of the elements in a script (setting, characters, dialogue, actions) needs to be considered carefully when you're writing your story.

Setting

The setting is the context where the action is taking place. This seems simple and obvious enough at first glance but when considered carefully, it's actually a very contextual piece of information. For example, imagine if somebody called you right now and asked, "Where are you?" How would you answer? It would depend on who was asking, when they were asking, and where the other person was.

When I was traveling frequently for work and it was known that I was often out of town, the answer might have been "San Francisco" to many of my friends. For a person who was local, the answer could have been a general "at work," comment, but if it was a colleague calling, then the answer would have been something much more specific such as "in conference room B."

In fact, the location alone may not be sufficient in a setting. I've been talking about setting as though it's only a place, but there's much more to context. Let's say I was in a car when someone called and asked, "Where are you?" Here are some answers I could give:

- "In a car" (somewhat useful but it doesn't describe much).

- "In a black Subaru" (might be completely unnecessary detail or might be incredibly useful if the person is on the lookout for your car).

- "On my way" (has similar utility to "in a car" in that it conveys you are in motion but not much else).

- "Almost there" (much more useful information, even though it's quite vague).

- "At 4th and Main" (more precise and useful, although not necessarily indicating whether you're staying there or not).

See how many ways you can establish a setting? Remember that who your audience is, how much they know, and how much you need them to know, all dictate how much information you need to include in the setting. Ask yourself these questions when you're determining the setting, but in addition to simply answering them, also answer "Is it important to state the following details?"

- Is it indoors or outdoors?

- Is it a place of work? Home? Other?

- What kind of building is it (for example, hospital, skyscraper, conference)?

- What city/country is it in?

- What time of day is it?

- What is the weather?

- What else is happening?

Let's sketch out a few of the Square scenarios we discussed in Chapter 4, "What's Your Comic About?" I talked about using a Square credit card reader at a local coffee shop, at a food cart vendor, or at a craigslist sale. So what happens if you don't take the time to establish a setting? Potentially, you could jump right into someone making a transaction with the Square device (see Figure 5.2).

However, without establishing a setting, you only know that a sale has taken place. For some scenarios, this might be perfectly sufficient, but it seems as if the story would be improved with some additional context. If you're creative with the way you build the comic, you could even show the setting without adding an additional panel. Let's change the comic to show a coffee shop as the setting (see Figure 5.3).

FIGURE 5.2
No setting established.

FIGURE 5.3
Coffee shop as setting.

With this simple change to the first panel, you've helped establish the setting without losing anything from the story. By the way, an opening panel like this is referred to as an *establishing shot* because it establishes the setting. In addition to using an establishing shot, you can also use another trick. Instead of adding a panel to show the merchant and customer conversing, you can implicitly associate the dialogue in the first panel. Although strictly speaking it might look like the building is talking, the reader can easily parse the real meaning if you make sure to continue the dialogue in the next panel. I'll talk more about this later in the chapter.

Showing the coffee shop from the outside is a very simple way of establishing the setting, but there are actually a lot of different ways you can accomplish the same thing. You can show the interior of the coffee shop from above, you can show a close-up of something representative of the setting, or you can even show a logo or sign that indicates the setting (see Figure 5.4).

FIGURE 5.4
Different ways to show a setting.

For each of these, you would describe the scenes differently in the script. Here are the four ways I've shown a coffee shop written in script form.

1.   SCENE: Exterior of the coffee shop, full view of the shop.

2.   SCENE: Interior of coffee shop, view from above.

3.   SCENE: Close-up of a cup of coffee being served.

4.   SCENE: Close-up of the coffee shop logo on a coffee cup.

All of them are effective and accomplish the goal of setting sufficient context. This is a great example of a case where there are many right answers. What method you choose to establish a setting can often be broken down to stylistic preferences. Experiment with different ways and see what you like.

A coffee shop works pretty well as a setting, but it doesn't quite highlight the strength of the product. You want to show that this product could be used *anywhere* and by *any business*, large or small. Instead of a coffee shop, you could explore more mobile settings, such as a food cart, shown in Figure 5.5. For that scenario, you might want to focus on the fact that it's a small business—tiny even—and you can establish this by showing the whole scene at once.

FIGURE 5.5
Food cart as setting.

To emphasize the size (or lack thereof), in this case, I focused on showing not only the merchant but also the environment around the cart. Showing other objects and people in the scene helps the reader get a sense of the scale. The mobile aspect is also highlighted by putting the food cart outdoors. The time of day, the specific intersection or park, and even the goods being sold aren't crucial to getting the point across.

Characters

Once you have a setting established, you can start to define the characters that will live in the setting. Several different types of characters that might exist in your story include the following:

- Characters that represent the people with the problem you're solving (the target audience).

- Characters that interact with the target audience.

- Objects or locations that play a significant role as a character (often the solution).

For the most part, you probably have an idea who these characters are already. Many companies will have marketing teams that research the market segmentation and demographics of your customers. User experience teams will often put together fictional personas that represent typical customer archetypes. These personas are chock-full of details not only about the age and gender of the person but also the habits and problems they typically run into.

If you don't have this sort of data available to you, I definitely recommend you spend some time doing some basic interviews of your potential market.

Your comic is a proposal. Basically, it's a story that explains how a product or service you're offering solves a problem for a specific kind of person. In order to use the comic to validate the idea, you'll need to know who to show the comic to!

As you decide on who your characters are and what they look like, remember that one of the advantages of comics is the ability to abstract the details of the characters. For example, if you're proposing a service that appeals to males 13–35 years old, you don't need to draw someone who is obviously one age or the other. A stick figure will often suffice.

For my Square example, I have three characters that are important: the merchant selling the goods, the buyer, and the Square reader.

Dialogue

I've talked about how comics are a unique juxtaposition of words and images. The dialogue in a comic represents a significant part of the "words" portion of comics. But is the dialogue anything more than words in speech bubbles, as represented in Figure 5.6?

FIGURE 5.6
Whoa!!!

Although most people will associate the imagery as the primary component of comics, the use of words in comics is just as much an art form—so much so that mainstream comics will often have a dedicated writer as well as a letterer—someone whose sole job is to write the words on the comic.

Even in the whimsical t-shirt above, there are a number of elements beyond the words, "Whoa!!! It's like I'm in a comic book."

The sizes of the words are varied to change the emphasis. Sure, there are three exclamation marks to really drive home the expression, but it's the size that really matters here.

The "Whoa!!!" is also placed in its own speech bubble, giving it additional emphasis but also setting up a pause. Earlier, I mentioned how comics can show the passage of time in very unique ways. One such method is with the placement and number of speech bubbles.

Finally, the words "comic book" are **bolded** to also show emphasis within the second speech bubble—but less emphasis than the oversized "Whoa!!!"

If you read superhero comic books such as *The Incredible Hulk*, you'll start to notice how each word is carefully crafted as though it were a piece of art in and of itself. In particular, action comics will use words as artistic sound effects represented through their lettering style (see Figure 5.7).

FIGURE 5.7
Lettering styles.

Not only can the text be stylized but even the container—the speech bubble—can use different styles to communicate different levels of emphasis. You're probably already familiar with a lot of the conventions without even realizing it. For example, a burst instead of a bubble often represents a loud noise or a yell. This convention is frequently used in supermarkets and other stores where you will see a "NEW!" or "SALE!" sign encapsulated.

Slightly less prevalent is the use of dotted lines to represent a whisper. A wavy, squiggly line might be used to convey something spooky and ethereal. A rigid, rectangular bubble may represent a robotic or computerized voice. Much like the font choices, the shape of the speech bubble can tell us a lot (see Figure 5.8).

FIGURE 5.8
Different speech bubbles can give different meaning.

Choosing Your Words Carefully

Of course, the visual style of the words and bubbles means little if the content isn't chosen carefully. Writing the dialogue can be the trickiest part of creating a believable and engaging comic. Before I talk about some guidelines, let's return to the Chapter 1, "Comics?!" example from Yahoo! When our team was creating this comic, we created a number of different characters, each with its own story.

One of our designers, Shane Kibble, created a character named George. In George's story, he was planning a trip and wanted to use our new features to create a personal map. For George, the ability to create his own paths and mark points of interest seemed like a great way to plan a backpacking trip. The feature was called *map annotations* and in the comic, there was one panel where George made the statement shown in Figure 5.9.

FIGURE 5.9
This is George.

We showed this comic, as well as the two other ones we made, to prospective users of the yet-to-be-built product. Our hope was to get a feeling of whether this was a problem that resonated with them. When we showed George's comic, these were some of the comments we received:

"His girlfriend must be really mad at him for him to go through all this trouble."

"This guy has no life."

"Wow! This guy is really anal."

It became clear that the language in this particular panel wasn't realistic, so we changed it to something with less jargon...but not before our poor fictional friend George was dubbed by the team as "Anal George."

Our lesson from that experience was to make sure that we used language that was fitting to the characters being portrayed. When you are trying to create a fictional story around a corporate message, it's very easy to forget to check the marketing messaging at the door.

It's also very easy to fall into the trap of being overly enthusiastic. Remember those radio advertisements where two people were talking to each other? For example:

ROGER

`"Hi, Jenny! What're you doing?"`

JENNY

`"Oh, I'm just looking at the classifieds trying to find a new place to live. My current place is` *horrible,* `but it's` *so hard* `to find anything."`

ROGER

`"Have you tried` *craigslist*`?"`

JENNY

`"No! What's that?"`

ROGER

`"It's a website where people post places for rent!"`

JENNY

`"WOW! Look at this. With` *craigslist,* `I'll have a new apartment in no time!"`

Despite being a completely fictional advertisement, just imagining this conversation coming up on the radio makes me shudder. I think people are very attuned to spotting what is and isn't genuine. Most of us are not actors, but we can spot bad acting. Similarly with the comic you write, it's very obvious when the dialogue is "Gee whiz! Isn't this a great product!" contrived to show off the product, as opposed to a believable story. There's no magical formula to ensure that your comic sounds realistic, but if you're building something that truly solves a problem, it shouldn't be too difficult. If you do find it difficult to create a story that isn't contrived, it might be a sign that the product itself isn't solving a realistic need!

Captions

So far, I've primarily talked about dialogue as it refers to the words within speech bubbles. Another important content piece is what's referred to as the *captions* in comics. Captions are frequently at the top or bottom of the panel and usually serve as some sort of narrative. You can see some example captions in Figure 5.10.

FIGURE 5.10
Examples of captions.

You can use captions to convey any information you want. They can be used to communicate time ("two hours later"), setting ("in a galaxy, far, far away"), action ("George studied the book in more detail"), or even dialogue ("George asked the man to stop"). Although you typically use speech bubbles to indicate dialogue, sometimes you may want to change perspectives so that the character is out of view. By keeping the dialogue in the caption, the reader can infer that it's still the same person talking, as shown in Figure 5.11.

FIGURE 5.11
Using (a) off-panel speech bubbles and (b) captions to continue dialogue.

In this example, the character is talking about her phone. The first panel establishes who is speaking and the context. In the second panel, you can see the phone close up but not the character. You can still use speech bubbles here, with the origin pointing off-panel to show it's still the same person speaking. Finally, in the last panel, you see a full view of the phone, and there is no room for anything else. Here, you might want to use the caption to show that the character is still speaking.

A few cues, such as the ellipsis from the previous panel and the quotation marks around the caption, help the reader connect this to the dialogue. You could actually use the caption to show dialogue in all three panels.

Because captions are so flexible, they are also the easiest element to abuse. When people show me the comics they've created for their organizations, the most common problem I see is an abuse of captions. Those poor, poor captions! So much is asked of them. Like in this story by Frank Ramirez, shown in Figure 5.12.

CD Conversion Service

Step 1
In her local retail store, Megan sees CD-Conversion Envelopes on display. Megan decides to give it a try.

Step 2
At checkout, Associate scans barcode on front of envelope. Upon purchase, envelope is "activated".

Step 3
When Megan gets home, she follows directions on the envelope and takes the CD booklets out of her CD cases. She counts the booklets, puts them in the envelope.

Step 4
Megan goes online to complete the purchase, selects file formats, and signs-up for a free account. She then drops the envelope in the mail.

Step 5
A few days later, she gets an email with a link to her entire collection online. She can now enjoy her music on many devices: computer, cell phone, and networked home audio gear!

FIGURE 5.12
So many captions!

Ramirez's comic does a good job of showing what this CD conversion service does, and it's certainly more interesting than marketing copy. However, it could be even better!

This story is essentially told entirely through the captions. If you look at Step 4, Megan is completing a purchase, signing up for an account, and even dropping an envelope off in the mail. That's a lot of steps that aren't represented by the art.

Could the story have been told instead through pictures and spoken dialogue? Why not just have Megan talk about her CD collection? How many of the words used in the captions could be illustrated or spoken instead?

The Story Is All Around You

Karl Dotter is a UX cartoonist. He founded ToastCo Labs to help companies visually explain how they work and why they matter. Here, Karl explains how you can generate characters and start forming stories without even writing a script.

At ToastCo we tell the best start-up stories. Working with Bolt Peters, we focused on crafting a story that included real motivations and desires that a researcher might have. These real-life ingredients help make the characters and story relatable to the reader. Sometimes a client has a great vision or script that they come to the table with, like Gerald the Researcher, a character Bolt Peters and ToastCo created for an animation describing their UX Research product, Ethnio.com. At the core of a good product, business, or comic is a human story. This story usually involves the daily pleasures and pains we can relate to in our lives. With Gerald, it was a very specific type of pain. Gerald was frustrated with the type of results he was getting with his research lab and so the visuals of Gerald wishing he was a hero of UX research matched his motivations, dreams, and desires. How realistic are the characters, locations, and actions in your story? Try focusing on these three aspects of the story and make them authentic so that readers can feel an "I relate to that" connection with the story.

Let's say you have that scribbled scenario and a character in mind. How would you do the storytelling part without ever using a script? Tom Hart, a former instructor at New York's School of Visual Arts, now at his own school, SAW, SequentialArtistsWorkshop.org, teaches cartooning to undergrads. He has a very simple process for collecting and generating story ideas. He first collects and writes down characters, locations, and actions on 3 x 5 index cards and puts them in an organized box. When he's ready to create a new story, he'll pick a character type, a location type, and an action type. This is a great method to create an instant story. I practice a similar technique by writing dialogue notes on one side of an index card and drawing a thumbnail of the scene or action on the other side. Very quickly you can start to organize a collection of these index cards into what can later become a storyboard or comic (Figure 5.13).

FIGURE 5.13
Collecting and
generating story ideas.

You can be a good storyteller. As you begin to practice creating and experimenting with characters, contexts and motivations, remember that there are stories all around you. Just the act of opening your eyes and ears and observing your surroundings is enough to start a great story.

Perhaps the defense of such lengthy captions is that it would be too cumbersome to draw a panel just to show Megan dropping off an envelope. I would suggest that this is precisely why you shouldn't rely on captions to carry a narrative.

By attempting to capture the story fully within the art and the dialogue, you force the question, "Do you want to spend time drawing this? Maybe it's not an important part of the story." The time and effort required to draw the extra panel can force you to focus on what information is truly important to convey. It may also force you to think about how much work you're putting the user through. If it's easier to not draw Megan with an envelope, think how much work it is for her to leave the house to actually physically do it!

Remember: *Don't use captions as a crutch* to add unnecessary information and always try to *speak from the character's voice*. The less you use narration and the more you embrace constraints, the more efficient your comic will be in doing its job.

How You Tell the Story

Constraints will force you to select a handful of core ideas and then find the most concise way to explain them. Another product that enforces constraints is Twitter because you're not allowed to have more than 140 characters in each message (or *Tweet*). When Twitter was first introduced, this limitation seemed like it would lead to inane messages about sandwiches, but as people became used to the medium, they started recognizing just how much could be said within 140 characters. I've found that my process for writing a Tweet and fitting it within the constraints is the same process I use to reduce my story to a comic.

When I write a Tweet, I first write exactly what I'm trying to say without any editing. Typically, this starts out longer than 140 characters. Through a few edits, I find that the character limit forces me to think about what the truly important and salient points are that I'm trying to make. This process I use for editing my Tweets is the same process you can use to edit your story and reduce it to its core.

Here's an example of a Tweet I was trying to write. I was visiting Lisbon for a conference and noticed that in many restrooms, very detailed, diagrammed instructions were posted on how to wash your hands. Why were such posters necessary? Was there a widespread problem with the technique in hand washing? Was it simply supplied by the government instead of "employees must wash their hands"? I had no idea. So I wrote this Tweet shown in Figure 5.14.

To be clear, I wasn't actually troubled by these signs. They're good reminders, and it's probably accurate to say that many people *don't* wash their hands thoroughly enough, but it was a message meant in jest. The Tweet is 151 characters so it's over the limit. Let's take a few different approaches to edit down the contents of the Tweet and compare that to how you might apply it to your comic story.

I keep seeing signs around Lisbon's restaurants that give detailed instructions on how to wash your hands. The necessity of these signs has me worried.

151

FIGURE 5.14
Initial Tweet.

Remove Unnecessary Details

The first thing you can do is remove descriptions, adjectives, and other notes that aren't important to the Tweet. The signage isn't exclusive to restaurants and even if it were, that point isn't important for this message. Nor is it important to specify "your" hands—only that there are signs for how to wash hands. These edits bring the Tweet down to 132 characters (Figure 5.15).

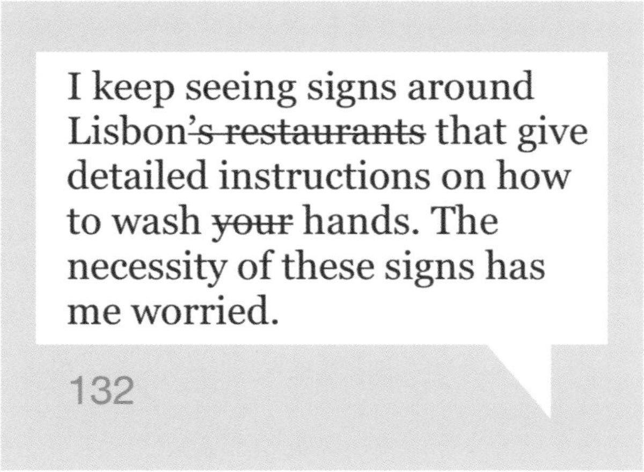

I keep seeing signs around Lisbon's restaurants that give detailed instructions on how to wash your hands. The necessity of these signs has me worried.

132

FIGURE 5.15
Remove unnecessary details.

The same can be applied to your comic story. The Square product accepts all major credit cards, including the usually less supported Discover and American Express cards. That could be considered a feature worth mentioning, but put into the context of a story about a credit card processing system that fits in your pocket, the exact details seem much more trivial. Simply mentioning "all major credit cards" would suffice.

Be Direct

So 132 characters is not bad, and it fits within the 140-character limit, but I thought I could do a lot better. Let's listen to our high school English teachers (or Microsoft Word) and switch out some of the sentence structure and use the active voice. I'll use "giving" instead of "that give," "hand washing instructions" instead of "instructions on how to wash hands," and "worries me" instead of "has me worried." And just like that, I have a 98-character Tweet (see Figure 5.16)!

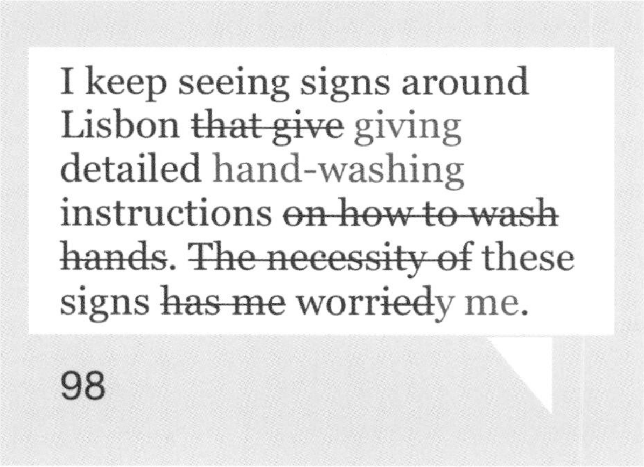

I keep seeing signs around Lisbon ~~that give~~ giving detailed hand-washing instructions ~~on how to wash hands.~~ ~~The necessity of~~ these signs ~~has me~~ worri~~ed~~y me.

98

FIGURE 5.16
Using the active voice solves the problem.

It's important to get right to the point in your comic, too. No panel should be wasted on anything other than conveying the use case for your product.

Combine Points

I'm doing pretty well now with the Tweet because 98 characters *are* concise and direct. Yet I think I can reduce the size even further by combining the two sentences. They're highly related, so why separate them? This brings the character count to 77 characters without losing any meaning (see Figure 5.17)!

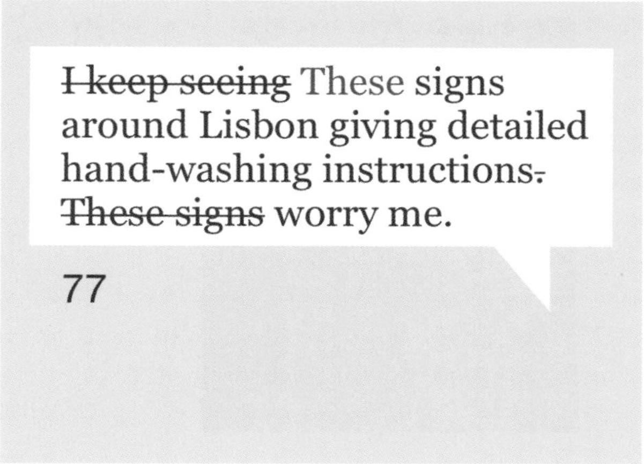
~~I keep seeing~~ These signs around Lisbon giving detailed hand-washing instructions~~.~~ ~~These signs~~ worry me.
77

FIGURE 5.17
Combine points.

Combining points is one of the most powerful things you can do with comics. A panel does not equal a single feature or action; it's a scene in and of itself that includes a background, a foreground, actions, dialogue, and even passage of time. Let's say it was actually important to showcase the specific credit cards that Square accepts. You can show, in one panel, how Square is a mobile payment system, it works on a phone, and it accepts every major credit card (see Figure 5.18).

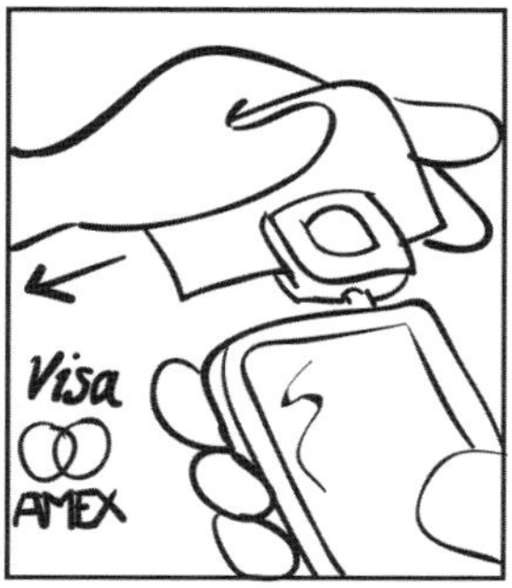
Visa
AMEX

FIGURE 5.18
You can combine points into one.

Show Don't Tell

At 77 characters, I thought I'd done pretty well, but Russ Unger, a fellow speaker at the conference in Lisbon, made the same observation about the hand-washing signs and had this to say in Figure 5.19.

FIGURE 5.19
Russ Unger's Tweet.

Not only did he manage to include the identifier of the conference "#uxlx" (which stands for User Experience Lisbon), but even with that, he was able to keep his Tweet down to 71 characters! The reason is because he didn't describe the signs, but simply attached a photo of one.

Comics are illustrative, as well as descriptive. Wherever possible, you should try to show the reader the subject rather than talking about it. Instead of saying it accepts all major credit cards, you can show the four company logos. Instead of talking about how portable it is, you can simply show it in use on a phone. In fact, some comics do such an incredible job of illustrating the point, they barely even require words to accompany it.

Writing the Square Script

Now that we've explored how to create a script for a comic, let's revisit the essential features we want to highlight with Square and determine an appropriate script:

- Free App on iPhone, iPad, Android.

- Free card reader device that plugs into the mobile device's headphones jack.

- Accepts Visa, Mastercard, American Express, Discover.

- Purchasers can use their fingers or a stylus to sign their signatures on the phone or iPad.

- The purchaser can get a receipt by email or text message.

- From the website, the vendor can track a history of all invoices.

Remember the properties of a story we care about are **setting**, **characters**, **actions**, and **dialogue**. Our setting could be a food cart, like I illustrated earlier in the chapter, but let's use another setting that is equally mobile and perhaps more accessible to professionals. In the last chapter, we decided that the story would be in the context of a tradeshow or conference. The specific tradeshow doesn't matter. In fact, it would probably be better not to use a real tradeshow name because that would alienate those who don't recognize it. Thus, our **setting** will be generically "tradeshow."

> SCENE: Exterior of a conference center. Sign reads "Annual Tradeshow"

As for the **characters**, we have two we care about: the merchant and the customer. We'll have the merchant sell books and call that person **Lou**. Presumably, the customer is someone attending the tradeshow and interested in the books for sale. We'll call this character **Nicole**.

The only thing left to determine will be the actions and dialogue. The story we want to tell is one where a customer is buying books from this merchant and uses Square to pay for it. The setting already helps establish how the product allows someone to accept credit cards from anywhere.

One way to start is by showing Nicole browsing through the books and then asking to purchase them. But instead of showing Nicole browsing, why not skip straight to the payment? If we start with Lou asking for a payment, the reader will infer that Nicole is interested in buying the books, and we can tell the story more efficiently.

> SCENE: Exterior of a conference center. Sign reads "Annual Tradeshow"
>
> LOU
>
> That'll be $60 for the two books.

Notice that the scene is showing the exterior of the conference center so you can't actually *see* Lou yet. We're both establishing the setting and starting the dialogue of the story. Through the next panels, the reader will figure out who's talking from the context.

Once Lou asks for the payment, we want to highlight that any major credit card is accepted. We also want to show the reader what the device looks like and how small it is. To do this, we should show a close-up of the reader and the phone.

SCENE: Interior of conference center in front of a book cart. Lou is standing with Nicole, who's holding two books.

NICOLE

Do you take credit cards?

LOU

Sure! Any card you like.

LOU *swipes Nicole's card through the Square reader*

Notice how we used dialogue to illustrate how any card was accepted. Sometimes, we can simply talk about the features. An alternative approach would be to show the credit card logos, but in this case, showing would involve a lot of logos and a few words are more efficient.

After the card has been swiped, we can reinforce how portable the solution is by showing the customer signing her signature on the phone. Once again, we can use dialogue to supplement this with additional information. In this case, we highlight how the merchant Lou can send a receipt digitally.

LOU *hands the phone to* NICOLE

LOU

Just use your finger to sign your receipt, and I can text or email it to you.

The last piece is to show how the merchant can review sales from a Web interface. We'll show this by cutting to a different scene, Lou's office, and bridging the two panels with a simple caption.

SCENE: Interior of an office. Lou is sitting in front of his computer, which shows some charts from Square.

CAPTION

Later…

LOU

Let's see how many books I sold today.

And that's it! We can tell from reviewing the script whether we've covered all the major features. The script acts as a great foundation for the comic we're going to draw. You can imagine how a comic like this could be used either to explain the idea of Square before it was built or to explain the product to potential merchants afterward.

Collaborative Experience Storyboarding

Craighton Berman is a product designer, illustrator, and creative director whose practice focuses on using visual thinking to shape ideas. His design work is in the permanent collection of the Art Institute of Chicago, and he contributes illustration work to Dwell, Details, and Core77. Craighton uses a process called Collaborative Experience Storyboarding, where he defines products and services with his clients by creating comics together.

What inspired you to try using comics?

I come from an industrial design background, where we are trained to rapidly visualize ideas for products. This skill is amazing for working through features and form, but often falls short in expressing broader experiences. In doing research on storytelling, we stumbled across a DVD-extra that revealed Pixar's unique collaborative approach to storyboarding. They treated movie storyboarding like a design process: brainstorming, critique, iteration, and a focus on getting all the details just right. The parallels to experience design are uncanny!

What's it like to create comics with your clients?

Typically, I use this process in a workshop setting where there might be a dozen clients with varied backgrounds. Despite the diversity of views, storyboarding becomes a common language for exploring ideas. Its flexibility allows it to be used in multiple ways: as a tool to think about the current experience of users, as a framework for brainstorming new ideas, and as a vehicle for shaping future experiences. This process lets them think broadly about opportunities, instead of generating a list of features. I've found that by having teams create storyboards together, it prompts decision-making and fosters clarity of a design vision.

How do you create the comics?

First, we identify a character and setting: who is this user and where does their experience take place? We try to make these as specific as possible and avoid generic marketing personas. We then try to tell this user's "current state" story: what is this experience like for them right now? We will collaboratively write this script on Post-It notes, with one piece of action per sticky (this allows everyone to contribute) and a small doodle of the scene.

Once completed, we can then visually analyze the experience to identify pain points or opportunities in the current experience. We will often tag these spots with small Post-Its, essentially creating a list of brainstorm-starters. Then we brainstorm dozens of ideas (visually) around each of these areas and then vote on our favorite ideas. The final challenge is to fit the best ideas back into the script. This forces everyone to make decisions on what the overall experience should be like, instead of ending with a laundry list of brainstorm ideas.

Once the teams are done, we pitch the comic to each other and critique the new experience, with the goal of providing feedback for iteration. All of this is done in a tight time limit of just a few hours—the power is in the iteration and experimentation. In the end, after a few days of this process, we've created dozens of scenarios for a new product or service. Each of these comics is essentially an "experience prototype," co-created with the team of people who will be deeply involved in implementing these ideas later, so everyone has a shared vision of what the experience should be like.

Summary

Before drawing comics, it can be helpful to define some elements of your story in words:

- The setting where the story is taking place.

- The characters (human or otherwise) involved in the story.

- The dialogue spoken between characters.

- The actions taking place in the story.

Once these elements are defined, you can organize them into a script similar in format to those used for movies or plays. The more detailed your script is, the easier it will be to create the comic (or give it to another person to create).

In addition to what the story is, you also need to consider how you're telling the story and whether you're telling it as efficiently as possible. You can combine multiple points into one panel, remove extraneous details, and focus on showing what's happening rather than telling in words. With some practice, you'll find that a lot of your story can be communicated with very few panels.

CHAPTER 6

Laying Out the Comic

THE NEXT STEP IN THE PROCESS IS LAYING OUT THE COMIC.

THIS PROCESS IS ALSO USED IN FILMS (CALLED *STORY-BOARDING*)

WHEN YOU'RE AWARE OF DIFFERENT TRICKS TO LAY OUT YOUR COMIC, IT CAN GO FROM BORING...

...TO REALLY INTERESTING.

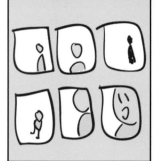

START WITH *COMPO-SITION*. INSTEAD OF ARRANGING THINGS IN THE MIDDLE...

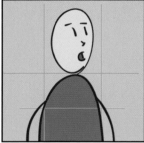

DIVIDING THE PANEL INTO *THIRDS* CAN BE MORE INTERESTING.

MAKE SURE TO LEAVE ENOUGH ROOM IN YOUR COMPOSITION, TOO.

UNLESS YOU'RE MAKING A POINT.

I'M SO LONELY...

YOU SHOULD ALSO WATCH OUT FOR INTERSECTING LINES.

EXIT

OR EVEN ADJACENT LINES THAT ARE TOO CLOSE.

YOU CAN ALSO VARY YOUR PERSPECTIVE. TREAT EACH PANEL LIKE YOU'RE LOOKING THROUGH A CAMERA.

LONG SHOTS ARE FARTHER BACK AND CAPTURE MORE OF A SCENE, SHOWING WHERE YOU ARE.

MEDIUM SHOTS ARE GOOD FOR SHOWING PEOPLE IN A SCENE.

CLOSE-UPS CAN BE USED TO HIGHLIGHT SOMETHING SPECIFIC...

YOU CAN COMBINE THESE TO "ZOOM IN" ON SOMETHING.

THE ANGLE YOU CHOOSE CAN CHANGE A SCENE, TOO.

LOW ANGLE SHOTS CAN MAKE YOU FEEL LIKE YOU'RE ACTUALLY THERE.

HIGH ANGLE SHOTS FEEL MORE DISTANT BUT GIVE AN OVER-VIEW OF THE SCENE.

POINT-OF-VIEW IS SEEING SOMETHING FROM THE PERSPEC-TIVE OF A CHARACTER.

EVEN WHEN YOU'RE SHOWING THE SAME THING...

...YOU CAN SHOW IT IN MANY DIFFERENT WAYS...

...TO MAINTAIN INTEREST.

LASTLY, KEEP IN MIND WHAT'S HAPPENING BEFORE AND AFTER A PANEL.

IF YOU KEEP CONTI-NUITY, REMEMBERING THINGS LIKE WHICH WAY PEOPLE WERE FACING...

RIIIING

THE READER CAN FOLLOW THE **FLOW** MORE EASILY.

O nce the comic's script is written, the next phase is to sketch out thumbnails of how to illustrate the story. This part of the process (Figure 6.1) isn't focused on the detailed art itself so much as on how the story is told.

FIGURE 6.1
Laying out the comic.

Think of it like a rough outline to base the final comic on—similar to what a wireframe is to a design. Through this outline, you should aim to answer the following questions:

- The **composition** of each panel: Where will you put your characters?

- The **perspective** you should draw from: Which way will your audience look at the characters?

- How the story is told in terms of the **flow** and **progression**: How will you change locations, show time passing, and detail movement?

This outlining process is often called *storyboarding* and is used frequently in film and design. Storyboarding is an art form that many people make entire careers out of, spending decades to perfect the art form. As such, it would be impossible for me to cover all the subtleties involved in storyboarding suffi- ciently...if I were storyboarding a film. Fortunately, I'm only trying to convey concepts in this chapter that would otherwise be described in thick market- ing assets, manuals, or requirements documents.

The techniques I describe in this chapter represent some pretty nuanced ele- ments of comic drawing. While there are a lot of different tips and tricks that can help make a comic more interesting or efficient, you shouldn't feel as if you have to remember or apply all of them right away. By simply being aware of them, you'll find yourself automatically applying many of the elements as your comic evolves. Here's an example in Figure 6.2 of how these techniques can make a story more interesting.

FIGURE 6.2
Two comics telling the same story.

Both comics tell the same story, but the second one uses many of the concepts I'm going to discuss. For example, the second comic uses more interesting perspectives that highlight the important parts of the story. It's also composed better, putting the words and characters in such a way that they don't seem crowded. Just as learning a few grammar rules of thumb can help improve writing, these techniques will help you create better comics with very little effort.

Composition

You'll often hear the term "composition" in relation to photography. In that context, composition refers to how you place all the elements in a photograph. Where is the subject? Where is the foreground and background? How do you arrange all of these in the most pleasing and interesting manner? Typically, these questions are answered in order to create an image that has visual unity—an image that doesn't seem jarring or uncomfortable to the eye. There are a multitude of composition techniques and guidelines that photographers use, and many of these same techniques apply to other visual arts as well, such as painting, design, and, of course, comics.

The Rule of Thirds

One basic guideline that is taught to beginning visual artists is "The Rule of Thirds." The premise behind the rule is that you can divide an image into thirds vertically and horizontally (see Figure 6.3). This division splits the image into nine equal parts. The goal is to put elements of the image near the lines. By doing so, you avoid putting the lines in the middle and cutting the image in half. Another way to look at it is to try and put the subject on one of the intersection points of the grid.

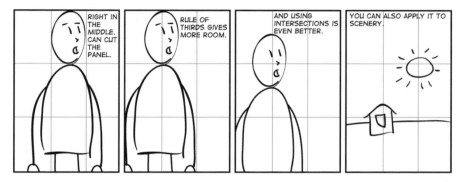

FIGURE 6.3
The rule of thirds.

In the example above, I put both the person and the house at intersection points. I also aligned some of the dominant lines with the grid. The Rule of Thirds isn't actually a rule so much as a guideline. This principle exists to discourage framing the subject in the center of a frame (or panel). Placing the subject at or near these intersections tends to create an interesting tension and draws the eye to the action. By putting lines along the grid, you also avoid bisecting the image.

Leave Enough Room

Carson Van Osten, a famous Disney artist, created something called the *Comic Strip Artist's Kit*. He drew this guide in 1975 to help artists avoid common mistakes. To this day, the points he made in that kit are as valid as ever. In the kit, Van Osten illustrates the frequent compositional problems that comic strip artists make, including cutting off the tops of characters with speech bubbles, or leaving too much space for the text and creating an awkward balance.

Most of the comics you draw will involve people and dialogue. When you start with the text and the speech bubbles, you'll find that the comic will look much more natural. Art and text that's overly crowded can be distracting or difficult to read, taking away from the message of the comic. Equally, you could end up in a scenario where you don't use enough of the panel and it looks particularly sparse. So you might want to lay out the dialogue first in order to see how much space you have left for the illustration, as shown in Figure 6.4.

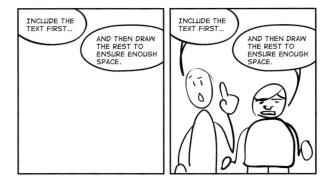

FIGURE 6.4
Include the dialogue first to help with composition.

On the other hand, you might actually *want* to convey a feeling of isolation or crowdedness. What if your product is designed to work even in very crowded spaces, such as public transit? Then you'd want to illustrate that point in that environment. However, if your product is designed to be used in open spaces, or perhaps creates that feeling, you would want to illustrate that as well (see Figure 6.5).

FIGURE 6.5
Deliberately making a panel crowded or sparse can create great results.

Intersecting Lines

When I'm discussing stick figure comics, talking about composition may seem a bit out of place. In fact, because we're using stick figures, a single line could mean anything from an arm to a chair to a beach. But as soon you put more than a person into a panel, composition becomes a bit more challenging. Each time a line intersects with another, you need to make sure it's clear what's going on. In the case of backgrounds, a very detailed background can often create clutter and obfuscate the subject of the comic. You can resolve this easily by breaking the intersections and creating a little bit of space between the background and the subjects, as shown in Figure 6.6.

FIGURE 6.6
Separating
background from
foreground.

Watch out, too, for instances where your lines are intersecting at almost the same angle. Lines overlapping each other are impossible to distinguish when you're dealing with stick figures. Usually, you can fix this simply by moving the character a little bit (see Figure 6.7). Alternatively, you can use some of the "fatter" stick figures we tried in Chapter 3, "You Don't Need to Be an Artist."

FIGURE 6.7
Overlapping lines and ways to avoid them.

Perspective

In film (and storyboards for films), there's the concept of *camera shots*. This term refers to where the camera is when filming a scene. The position of the camera can change how much information is revealed, what the viewer focuses on, and even what emotional reaction it elicits. Although your comic may not be a storyboard for a blockbuster film, the concept of camera shots still applies. If you view each panel as a television or movie screen, there is an imaginary camera that creates the image you're looking at (see Figure 6.8).

FIGURE 6.8
Each panel is like looking through a camera.

Like composition, the selection of camera shots can have a significant impact on how a story is told. Do you choose to frame the entire scene from a distance? Do you illustrate it head-on or at an angle? What angle? Each of these answers can create a very different mood and story. Camera shots change based on distance and angle. By changing these two variables, you will get dozens of different ways to illustrate a scene. Don't try to memorize all of these shots. What's more important is simply knowing such a variety exists so you can experiment with how you tell your story when you draw your comic later.

Distance

When you take a picture and you want to get more in the shot, you either zoom out or step back. The same concept applies to comics. The farther away the camera is, the more you can capture. In the last chapter, I talked about how you may need to use the first panel to establish the setting. In order to capture the whole setting, for example to see the entire coffee shop, you may need to have the "camera" set farther back. In film, these shots are called *long shots*. Closer shots, such as the one showing the cash register, are called *medium shots*. Check out Figure 6.9 for examples of both these shots.

FIGURE 6.9
The settings from Chapter 5, "Writing the Story," in film terms: long shot and medium shot.

Capturing a lot in a panel can be useful, but it can also make it hard to know what to focus on. The closer you are, the stronger the connection the reader has with the subject. If long shots answer the question, "Where am I?" then medium shots answer "Who is here?" or "What are they doing?" Medium shots are great for showing people in a scene. They are also appropriate for showing actions taking place between two people. Some examples of panels that use medium shots include the following shown in Figure 6.10:

- "Jason passed a $5 bill to Amy."

- "Ed is talking."

- "Patricia answers her phone."

FIGURE 6.10
Some examples of medium shots.

Moving closer than the medium shot, you get the *close-up*. That's when your panel is almost entirely filled with the subject. This close-up could be of a hand, a face, a phone, a flower, or anything you want the reader to look at and really see. It's great for showing static detail, such as the writing on a screen; more detailed motions you wouldn't see from a medium shot, such as finger movement; or to focus on a detail of a character, such as a character's facial expression. Often, when creating comics for products, there are specific details you want to focus on, so you might use a close-up for a panel or two. Examples of things you might want a close-up of include the following and are shown in Figure 6.11:

- "There's a receipt on the screen."

- "George swipes his finger across the phone."

- "Janey is contemplating what to buy."

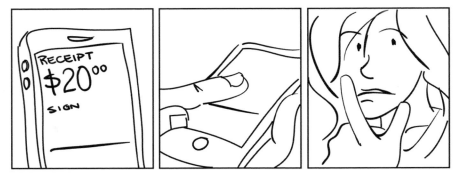

FIGURE 6.11
Some examples of close-ups.

You can also use a combination of these shots. In the comic book about risk management, *Commitment,* shown in Figure 6.12, the artist opens the scene with a long shot that shows a London landmark. This illustrates the city as well as a specific area: the financial downtown district. They then show an interior scene of an office, as though they were zooming in.

All these terms may seem overwhelming initially, but you'll be surprised how naturally you incorporate these concepts once you draw the comics. In many cases, it becomes very apparent immediately when you choose a shot that is or is not a good fit for the scene.

FIGURE 6.12
Zooming into a scene.

Angle

Aside from how far away the camera is, you can also change the angle of the camera. Imagine you were looking at a person and didn't move closer or farther away. Instead, you sat down. The person you were looking at now looks very different—perhaps more dominating and certainly more present. And if you were to get on a ladder, the angle would change again. The person would look smaller, perhaps less significant, and you could see more of the surroundings (see Figure 6.13).

FIGURE 6.13
Looking at a person from different angles.

There are four angles that you will find particularly helpful: eye-level, high angle, low angle, and point of view. For most scenes and by default, a scene is drawn at eye-level. That's what a scene would look like if you were looking at it from standing height. Or if you were looking at a scene where the subjects were sitting, then eye-level would refer to the sitting height. Sometimes, you'll want to create more interest in the scene and one of the other angles will then be more appropriate.

I mentioned that bringing a subject into close-up is a great way to engage your readers and have them focus on something specific. Another way of bringing the reader into the scene is to use a low-angle shot. This shot shows the reader looking up at the subject, which gives a more direct "I am actually *there* in the scene" feeling for the reader. Lower angles emotionally bring the user closer to the action depicted.

Conversely, high-angle shots, sometimes called *bird's-eye view shots*, create a more distant feeling. They show more of an overview of the scene, highlighting what's out there. That shot also creates a feeling of superiority or a feeling of smallness in the subjects. It's an angle that people are not generally accustomed to seeing, so there's less connection to the individuals in the scene. However, there are times when you want to have less connection and more focus on the scene itself. I used a high-angle shot in the previous chapter to show the interior of the coffee shop because it allowed the readers to see the entire coffee shop. Notice how a low-angle shot wouldn't have worked for this particular scene (see Figure 6.14).

The last angle that you'll use often is called *point-of-view*. As the name implies, this shot occurs when the angle of the camera is seen through the eyes of the character, which means the reader sees what the character sees. You'll probably find yourself using this a lot, because what the character is looking at is usually a computer or mobile screen. Aside from providing a convenient shot of the screen, point-of-view shots also connect the reader to the character, creating a feeling of *being* that person. Because the shot focuses on what the character is looking at, you'll find many close-up shots are also point-of-view shots (see Figure 6.15). In fact, it would be pretty strange *not* to have some shots be from the point-of-view of the character.

FIGURE 6.14
The view of the coffee shop interior was high angle instead of low angle.

FIGURE 6.15
Comparing a close-up using point-of-view and one that doesn't.

Selecting a Variety

So now you know that having the camera at different distances shows different amounts of information and creates different levels of engagement. You also know that changing how high you put the camera can impact the shot. These two variables create a lot of possible combinations in shots. How do you find the perfect shot for a given panel? The answer is that there isn't one perfect shot. Just as different film directors have different styles, how you draw your comic is up to you, and there is more than one correct answer.

Sometimes, it isn't even about the right shot so much as it is about mixing things up a bit. Changing shots in a comic can be useful simply to avoid monotony. If you've ever watched a daytime soap opera, you'll know how the "talking head syndrome" can become incredibly dull. The camera alternates between two characters' heads and very little of the scene changes for a long period of time. The same can happen in comics when the story involves a lot of talking. Comic artist Wally Wood was so sick of receiving scripts that involved pages upon pages of talking heads that he developed a little cheat sheet for himself called *Wally Wood's 22 Panels That Always Work*. If you search for that online, you'll probably find some reproductions of it. I can't show it to you here, but here's a re-creation of a few of the panels to give you an idea (Figure 6.16).

FIGURE 6.16
Kevin Cheng's simulation of Wally Wood's *Panels That Always Work*.

What Wally Wood shows his audience is that you can make a scene interesting simply by changing the shots. There are examples of this in film as well. A classic film, *12 Angry Men*, involves 12 jurors deliberating over a murder case. The film is almost entirely shot in the jury deliberation room—a small conference room. Through creative camera shots, masterful performances, and an engaging script, the filmmakers kept the viewer interested in the movie. Imagine how much harder it would have been for the actors if the movie were shot from the same angle throughout!

Depending on the product you're trying to conceptualize, you may find yourself faced with similar challenges of repetitiveness. With the Square comic, we had a product that was being used out in the world, so there was a fair bit of variety in the scene and some interaction between characters. With many other applications, especially Web-focused products, you'll find yourself repeatedly drawing a person in front of a computer.

In these instances, utilizing different camera angles can be an easy way to keep it interesting. Be careful, though, because changing camera shots for the sake of changing them can often be jarring for your readers and make it difficult for them to follow the sequence. Make sure when you change shots that your reader can still follow the action. In particular, pay special attention to clarify who is speaking.

Wally Wood created variety by changing the angle, using tricks like silhouettes, close-ups, and cropping to create interest in a scene. Let's borrow his approach to create some panels to be used for scenes with computer products. There are a surprising number of ways you can show a person in front of a computer—focusing on the person, the screen, or a combination.

Let's start with a few templates that focus on the character's face alone. Back in Chapter 3, I talked about how abstraction can be used to take away details and let the reader fill in the blanks. I also touched upon how the user interface can and should be abstracted so as to focus the reader on the story. Here are a few ways you can show a person using a computer but not show the interface (see Figure 6.17).

FIGURE 6.17
Panels showing character using a computer.

These are pretty basic templates. For a little variety, you can also show the character without showing his face. Showing the face is useful to either establish the character ("Who is this?") or to see some expression on his face. Once you've done so, a subsequent panel can be made more interesting by changing the shot. You can show a silhouette of the character, show the scene from their back, or show it through a window (see Figure 6.18).

FIGURE 6.18
Panels showing the character without showing the face.

Design Promos Like Comic Book Panels

Jenni Chasteen is a freelance blogger (http://jenniart.com/), *Web designer, and self-described geek who spends as much of her time doodling as she does designing. She wrote a piece for* Inspired Magazine *on "How Comics Can Make You a Better Designer"* (http://inspiredm.com/comic-books-design/). *With their permission, I've included a segment from the article on making layouts more interesting.*

While I was working as the assistant graphic designer at a large ecommerce company, I'm pretty sure I was the reason the Senior Graphic Designer had ulcers. It's not that I intentionally set out to irritate her; it's just that we didn't always see eye-to-eye on design choices. She came from a Web graphics/marketing background, and I came from more of a self-taught/animation-school drop-out/good-at-BSing-my-way-through-life background. When she designed things, she designed them with a strict level of symmetry and order. When I designed things, I tried to never do the same thing twice.

On one occasion, I handed in a mock-up of two adjacent promos, one with a close-up of a product, and one that was zoomed out. When she reviewed it, she told me to make them both the same size.

Thinking that my design philosophy was incredibly clever, I began to explain, "Well, I learned in storyboard class that no two panels in a comic should look the same…"

"This isn't a comic book. It's a website."

I was trying to explain that two side-by-side panels with two characters that are the same size in the same place look homogeneous, causing both of them to get overlooked. The same could be said for adjacent promos.

The homepage of the website we worked on together had a grid of ever-changing promos featuring different products. These weren't very interesting products, so we had to do what we could to make the site look interesting. For argument's sake, let's say the products were cheese graters.

If you place a row of ads with identical layouts together, the viewer doesn't see anything special about them…they just see a row of the same thing like in Figure 6.19.

FIGURE 6.19
Advertisements with identical layout.

Imagine that same format in a comic book, as in Figure 6.20. It doesn't work does it?

In fact, in a comic book, you expect to see different-sized elements with different placement. You see a clear difference between each panel, and it's a helluva lot more interesting to look at something like Figure 6.21.

So why is it that we expect to see conformity in promos? By switching close-ups with full shots and using varied text placement, you get an exceptionally different final result. Each promo in Figure 6.22 conveys a unique message while standing out from the others. Careful use of fonts and colors can still give them cohesion without appearing identical.

FIGURE 6.20
Comic book with identical layout.

FIGURE 6.21
Different sized elements and placement in a comic.

FIGURE 6.22
Varied shots and placement in promotions.

Sometimes, you might want to show just a little portion of the interface—enough to give the readers some context. For example, you may want to illustrate that a person is on a particular website. ("Zoe is searching for something on Google.") You can show this by talking about Google explicitly, but a more elegant solution might be to show the logo of the site on their screen—just enough context to serve your needs.

If you determine that you do need to show some of the interface, there are a number of ways you can do so (see Figure 6.23). You can show a cropped part of the screen, over the shoulder of the character. Alternatively, you can show the hands of the character and the bottom of the screen. This shot gives some variety to the comic and also helps communicate when the character is typing something. Finally, my favorite variation is not to show the interface on the screen at all, but instead to show it overhead—like a speech bubble for the computer.

FIGURE 6.23
Panels showing some interface.

These templates I've shown are my version of Wally Wood's panels that are re-created for human-computer interaction. Collectively, they provide you with an easy reference for composition ideas when you create your comic. The concepts behind them also apply to mobile phone usage. You can show someone on a phone without any interface, silhouettes of a person, or close-ups of them using the phone. I've collected these examples and created full templates—both for computer and mobile devices—in the appendix, "Useful Templates and References." When you need some ideas on how to lay out your comic, you should refer to these templates as a starting point.

Flow and Progression

Before we wrap up with the Square example, I'd like to touch on the flow of a comic. I've mentioned how comics can represent time and movement powerfully. However, using this strength effectively can be challenging. So far, I've talked mostly about how each individual panel should look. But comics are about sequential art, and *how* you sequence can matter just as much as what is in the sequence.

The most important aspect to consider in regard to flow is this: Does the reader know what happened between two panels? If you can always address this, your comic will be understandable. Often, the key is providing enough context in one panel to make sense of the next. For example, if you want to show characters using their phones, then show them holding the phones in the previous panel. There are also subtle details that can go a long way. Keeping details consistent from panel to panel, such as which side the character is standing in relation to others, what hand they're using, and so on, is crucial (see Figure 6.24).

FIGURE 6.24
Flow with (a) no context (b) flipped sides.

Panels in a comic are intrinsically linked together. Each panel doesn't stand alone. When you consider each panel, look at its neighbors and whether they link to each other well. If you treat them like words in a sentence or paragraphs in an essay, you'll find it fairly easy to tie them together. The best way to test your flow is to have someone else look at your comic, without the words, and see if that person can determine what order to read your comic.

Laying Out the Square Script

Now that you've seen all the ways to lay out a comic, let's take a look at the script we completed in the last chapter and see if we can apply some of the lessons to our example. Here's the script:

> **SCENE: Exterior of a conference center. Sign reads "Annual Tradeshow"**
>
> **LOU**
>
> That'll be $60 for the two books.
>
> **SCENE: Interior of conference center in front of a book cart. Lou is standing with Nicole, who is holding two books.**
>
> **NICOLE**
>
> Do you take credit cards?
>
> **LOU**
>
> Sure! Any card you like.
>
> LOU *swipes Nicole's card through the Square reader*
>
> LOU *hands the phone to* NICOLE
>
> **LOU**
>
> Just use your finger to sign your receipt, and I can text or email it to you.
>
> **SCENE: Interior of an office. Lou is sitting in front of his computer that shows some charts from Square.**
>
> **CAPTION**
>
> Later…
>
> **LOU**
>
> Let's see how many books I sold today.

Now let's break this script down into what it might look like in comic panels. First, let's look at what scenes are in the comic. There are three scenes: the exterior of the conference center, the interior of the conference center, and Lou's office. In each of these scenes, you need to decide how to lay them out. Let's start with the conference center exterior. The first thing I'm going to do is just try drawing a generic big glass building (see Figure 6.25a). As we'll discuss in the next chapter, it's OK to cheat a little and look at Google Images and other sites to see what conference centers look like.

Now, I could draw this building from any number of angles, but I want to make sure that the reader feels like they're there and not in a helicopter so I'll use a slightly lower and closer angle (Figure 6.25b). Finally, it still looks like a generic building so maybe we can add a little bit of context to the building by giving it a sign (Figure 6.25c). By the way, one of the best things about drawing comics is that you get to be an architect, an interior designer, a hairstylist, and a fashion designer. You can create whatever styles of buildings, offices, hair, and clothing you want!

FIGURE 6.25
A conference center (a) from above, (b) from a better angle, and (c) with some more context.

Now we've established the setting. The reader knows where this story is taking place, so we can transition to the next scene, the interior of the conference center. But what do we show? Should we show the whole conference interior? It seems from the script that it's some tradeshow floor we're showing. We could provide that context by showing a high-angle shot, but that's a lot of work for not much benefit. We already established that it's in a conference hall, and the conversation probably provides enough context. Let's instead focus on the interaction between Lou and Nicole (Figure 6.26a).

We can add more to the scene to provide more color. For example, we can add a table and some books to show that Lou is selling at some kind of booth (Figure 6.26b). We can also add some hint of people in the background to illustrate that it's a busy tradeshow floor (Figure 6.26c).

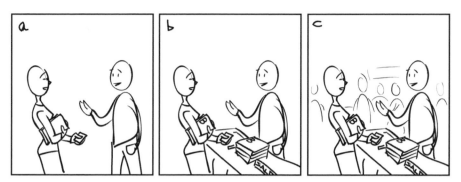

FIGURE 6.26
Interior of conference, (a) Lou and Nicole interacting, (b) with more context, and (c) some background activity.

After Nicole confirms that she can pay by credit card, she has to hand Lou her card, Lou has to swipe it through the Square reader, hand her the phone, and have Nicole sign it. We can illustrate this entire process step-by-step (Figure 6.27), but it gets rather tedious, not to mention boring to read.

FIGURE 6.27
The step-by-step transaction.

This level of detail seems rather laborious and excessive. What if we skipped a few steps, but made sure we still had enough context? It's not really necessary for us to show Nicole handing her card over, as the conversation implies she's the one paying. However, we do want to make sure to show Lou swiping the card, because we want to highlight the product and its size. So let's show an extreme close-up of him swiping the card (Figure 6.28a). After swiping the card, instead of having Nicole sign the receipt on the phone, we can use dialogue to explain what she'll be doing. If we use an angle that shows both Lou and the screen, we implicitly show the reader that the receipt can be signed on the phone (Figure 6.28b)!

FIGURE 6.28
Cutting the transaction
scene down by half.

So far, we've been looking at the scenes but not really considering the dialogue. If we look at the dialogue thus far, it goes like this:

LOU

That'll be $60 for the two books.

NICOLE

Do you take credit cards?

LOU

Sure! Any card you like.

LOU

Just use your finger to sign your receipt, and I can text or email it to you.

Drawing out the entire dialogue panel by panel would look like Figure 6.29.

FIGURE 6.29
The scene's dialogue.

It's better, though, to combine this dialogue with the scenes we've already created. Remember that you don't need to always show the face of the person speaking, provided you give enough context either before or after the panel to infer who is speaking. So we can actually start Lou's dialogue from outside the conference center in the first panel. When we switch to the interior of the conference center, Nicole is responding to Lou, and that's clear from the flow of conversation (the person saying it's $60 wouldn't also be the person asking if credit cards were accepted). In the second panel, we can also combine Nicole's question with Lou's response. Finally, in the last panel, Lou can ask Nicole to sign the receipt in the scene where he's handing the phone to her. Figure 6.30 illustrates these changes.

And that's the conference scene in four panels! Notice I did make one little tweak. I saw that the close-up to the card swipe panel seemed a bit abrupt since no phone was visible beforehand, so I have Lou already holding the phone with the square device in the previous panel. It's a subtle detail, but these are the things you'll notice as you put the story together. Make sure that everything flows together cohesively!

FIGURE 6.30
The conference scene with dialogue included.

Finally, we have another scene transition where we show Lou back at his office. Once again, we consider what's important to show in the scene to help us decide what angle to use. In this case, we want to show that he's in his office, at his computer, and show enough of the screen to indicate that Square is giving him information about sales numbers. Let's show him from behind, sitting at a computer. We'll reveal enough of the screen to show he's on Square's website and looking at some charts.

And with that, we have a rough cut of the whole comic (see Figure 6.31)!

FIGURE 6.31
A comic depicting Square being used.

Summary

In this chapter, we talked about how to compose a panel in a way that clearly highlights your story without unnecessary noise and distractions. We also talked about how different camera angles can create different effects and be used to help convey your messages more effectively. Finally, we looked at how the combination of panels can be put together to create a cohesive flow.

- **Composition:** Use the Rule of Thirds, leave enough room for dialogue, and avoid intersecting lines.

- **Perspective:** Adjust distance depending on how much of the scene and the level of detail you want to show; adjust the angle to change how the reader relates to the scene.

- **Flow and Progression:** Keep in mind the context of adjacent panels and remember that comics are called *sequential* art.

We also took the example Square script to the next step and figured out how best to lay out the comic. We've largely been talking about doing all of these comics using stick figures, and the comic we did at the end of this chapter may be sufficient to illustrate Square's product use case. However, it's possible to create more complex art without a lot of effort. There are so many tools and tips out there these days, you can easily create higher fidelity comics yourself, and that's what we're going to cover next.

CHAPTER 7

Drawing and Refining

NOW THAT WE HAVE SOME LAYOUTS, LET'S TALK ABOUT SOME RESOURCES TO HELP WITH FINISHING TOUCHES.

THE MOST USEFUL TOOL WE FORGET WE HAVE IS *TRACING*. YOU CAN TRACE ANY-THING...

...LIKE PHOTOS!

YOU CAN FIND ALMOST ANYTHING ON IMAGE SEARCHES TO TRACE.

THERE ARE ALSO *AVATAR GENERA-TORS* LIKE *YAHOO! AVATARS* THAT LET YOU CUSTOMIZE A CARTOON PERSON.

SITES LIKE YAHOO! AND *IMVU* HAVE MANY OPTIONS FOR CLOTHES AND POSES.

BUT BE CAREFUL SINCE THEY HAVE LIMITATIONS.

IF YOU USE THEM, I'D STILL SUGGEST TRACING ON TOP.

ASIDE FROM AVATARS, THERE ARE ALSO *SCENE GENERA-TORS* LIKE *STORY-BOARD ARTIST* AND *SECOND LIFE*.

3D ENVIRONMENTS AND MODELS CAN FEEL VERY ARTIFICIAL, THOUGH.

PROGRAMS LIKE *POSER* HELP, AS THEY LET YOU POSE PEOPLE HOWEVER YOU WANT.

BUT AGAIN, USING THESE AS REFER- ENCES FOR TRACING IS PROBABLY BEST.

SOME PEOPLE HAVE MADE FREE *COMIC TEMPLATES* YOU CAN USE!

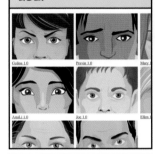

MARTIN HARDEE'S *DESIGN COMICS*, FOR EXAMPLE, HAS A LOT OF VARIETY.

THOUGH THEY CAN BE A BIT *TOO* REAL- ISTIC AND LOSE THE ABSTRACTION COMICS HAVE.

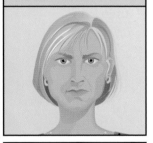

ANOTHER SET IS THE TOY COMIC KIT FROM BRYCE JOHNSON.

THEY'RE MADE FROM TOYS, SO THE ABSTRACTION IS STILL THERE!

ASIDE FROM DRAW- ING, THERE'S ALSO SOFTWARE TO HELP LAYOUT COMICS.

MANGA STUDIO LETS YOU EASILY REFINE DRAWINGS, ADD COLORS, EF-FECTS, AND LAYOUT.

AN EVEN SIMPLER (AND CHEAPER) LAYOUT TOOL IS **COMIC LIFE 2**.

IT ALSO COMES WITH SOME FUN FONTS, AND SPEECH BUBBLES.

THERE ARE A FEW ONLINE TOOLS YOU CAN USE. ONE IS CALLED **BITSTRIPS**.

THEY HAVE A LOT OF BUILT-IN CHARACTERS AND SCENES YOU CAN DROP IN.

YOU CAN EVEN CREATE YOUR OWN TO REUSE.

MY FAVORITE ONLINE TOOL IS **PIXTON**.

THEIR ART STYLE IS EASIER ON THE EYE AND I FOUND IT EASIER TO USE.

BUT Y'KNOW WHAT? DRAWING STICK FIG-URES IS STILL THE FASTEST WAY!

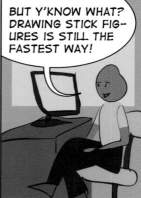

In Chapter 3, "You Don't Need to Be an Artist," we covered a lot of different techniques and basics for drawing stick figures and basic objects. We also talked about how to use just a few lines to suggest a character's body language and expression. These techniques are a great foundation for illustrating your product ideas, but comics have become so widespread as a technique that there is now a plethora of resources to help you create even better comics, faster. And you *still* don't need to know how to draw! So let's talk about the last step of drawing comics—the actual drawing (see Figure 7.1).

FIGURE 7.1
The last step is to draw your comic!

Now that we have some comics laid out, I'll cover some resources I've found to help you put the finishing touches on your comics. The resources are divided into the following categories:

- **Reference materials:** These are sites and tools you can refer to in order to help you draw something more complex.

- **Templates:** Over the past few years, a number of people have created and shared some useful templates from which you can create comics without drawing a single thing.

- **Comic creation software:** In addition to traditional drawing programs, there are a few specialized pieces of software for helping comic creators. Some of them emphasize layout, while others make the drawing process easier.

- **Online creation tools:** The rising popularity of comics has created a market for online services that let you create comics on their site, with no drawing necessary.

Some of these tools are incredibly powerful, and it's tempting to use them even if you don't need to. I deliberately left discussion of these resources until later so that you could understand first what your needs are and how to use tools appropriately to help accomplish those goals.

For example, if you're looking to quickly illustrate a use case to a colleague, it would take you a couple of hours at most with a few stick figures. In contrast, if you were to use some of these templates or comic generation tools, you might become so mired in the features that you would lose sight of what you were trying to communicate. "Look! Pixton lets me drop in pregenerated background such as trees and buildings! I'll just put a few of these in here." When this happens, you're letting the tools rule you instead of the other way around. You should already know what you need and then find the tool that matches. "I need this scene to be in a park and show some trees, so Pixton would be perfect for this."

Reference Materials

Remember Gordon McKenzie's story in *Orbiting the Giant Hairball* (refer to Chapter 3) where he discovers the number of artists dramatically decreased from kindergarten through elementary school? When I was a kid, I drew a lot and didn't stop to worry about how people viewed the quality of my art. I also did a lot of tracing of everything from photographs to my favorite comics. I would show these tracings with pride, without any sort of worry that I'd be judged because the work was not original.

Tracing is one of the quickest and most effective methods for creating comics. All the templates, tools, and reference materials that I mention in this chapter become even more useful when you include the option to trace over them.

Photographs

If you want to have a comic where you're showing somebody holding a phone, how do you know what that looks like? You might hold up the phone yourself and look at where the hand is, where the thumb is, and where it's being held in relation to the body. An easier way would be to take a photograph of somebody holding a phone and then try tracing it, as shown in Figure 7.2.

Tracing photographs is a great way to get exactly the imagery you want, especially for poses you might otherwise have trouble drawing. Even if you're more experienced and don't require tracing, finding or taking photographs to reference is a common technique used by professionals. In a comic I did a few years ago, there was a scene where I wanted to feature the U.S. Department of Defense headquarters, the Pentagon. Aside from knowing the shape of the building, I really didn't know what it looked like. So I found a photo of it and traced the outline, and then I filled in a few details by referencing the photo (see Figure 7.3).

FIGURE 7.2
Photo and tracing of someone holding a phone.

FIGURE 7.3
Photo and illustration of the Pentagon.

Thanks to the wonders of the Internet, you now have a plethora of image resources you can search to find appropriate images: Google Images, Flickr, stock art sites such as Getty, and of course, your own camera. Just make sure if you're using any images for actual distribution or marketing that you're following copyright laws.

You might think, "Well if I'm taking photographs of the poses already, why even trace them? I can just use the photographs, add some captions, and *voila*, I have a comic!" While this is true, you do encounter a few problems creating a comic this way, as shown in Figure 7.4.

FIGURE 7.4
Example of a photo-graphed comic.

With photograph comics, the characters in the comics are often of people on your team. The readers of your comic are often other members of the team—people who are likely to recognize the characters in the comic. This familiarity can distract the reader from the story at hand. "Hah, look at Kevin posing by the water cooler like a goofball." That isn't the first reaction you want to elicit from your comic.

Further, as discussed in Chapter 2, "Properties of Comics," one of the strengths of comics is their ability to abstract the irrelevant details, allowing the reader to focus on the use case. Instead of a representation of a person who the reader might be able to relate to, the story is now of a very specific person with no ambiguity.

Tracing a photograph allows you to select which details are important, while still using the photograph as reference material. In the tracing I did of me holding a phone, I didn't trace every detail. I didn't trace the background, every detail in the clothing, or even the face. I only used the details that mattered to me: the pose.

The wonderful thing about embracing tracing as a tool is that you're not limited to just photographs. There are many character and scene generators that may not be appropriate for creating a comic but can be great starting points to trace from.

Avatar Generators

One of these tools is Yahoo! Avatars.[1] Soon after we first used comics at Yahoo! Local, another team at Yahoo! approached me to show me a comic they had created to illustrate their story. To my surprise, the story was created using Yahoo! Avatars. If you're unfamiliar with it, Yahoo! Avatars is a tool that lets you customize a character—presumably to your likeness. The avatar can have different skin color, eyes, mouth, facial expressions, clothing, accessories, and even background.

I thought this was an incredibly creative way of creating a higher quality comic without doing any art. Exploring the tool further, I decided to create a few different versions of me, ranging from Casual Kevin to B-Boy Kevin to Depressed East Coast Kevin and finally to Pimp Daddy Kevin. As you can see from Figure 7.5, the range of the tool was quite vast!

FIGURE 7.5
Sample of Yahoo! Avatars.

Yet despite all of these options, I still found a few limitations. The avatars weren't able to do anything but stand in the same position, which greatly limited the expressiveness of the story. Remember how the body language can communicate so much about a character? With these characters, there is no body language other than staring straight at the reader.

Although Yahoo! Avatars has a wide range of backgrounds and styles available, you are still limited as to what is there. This limitation applies to all of these generators. If you were to use a tool like this to create your comics and found a scene that wasn't available, you'd *really* be stuck because now you would have to create something in the style of Yahoo!'s art or worse, limit or change your story to fit what's available.

---

1   http://avatars.yahoo.com

I recommend using something like Yahoo! Avatars only as a starting reference, rather than the tool to generate the comics themselves. Instead, trace over the images so that you have more flexibility to add to the library or change things.

Beyond Yahoo! Avatars, there are a lot of other similar generators available both as Web applications and purchased software. For example, IMVU[2] offers a lot of flexibility and customization options, and their avatars are in 3D (see Figure 7.6).

FIGURE 7.6
IMVU avatars.

Today, many sites offer some level of customization and many of those, such as Microsoft's X-Box gaming console, offer avatar creators. Any of these can be used to generate cartoon renditions of characters.

Some applications and sites offer more than just avatar generation. They allow you to create full scenes, including the character's poses.

Scene Generators

One tool that seems perfectly named for creating comics is *StoryBoard Artist*.[3] It's a downloadable tool for PC or Mac designed for cinematic storyboarding. That means the software is designed for storyboarding a movie before filming. While the audience target is different, storyboarding *is* storyboarding.

---

2 http://imvu.com

3 http://www.powerproduction.com/artist.html

The software has pregenerated characters, interiors, exteriors, and props that you can place (as shown in Figure 7.7). And unlike Yahoo! Avatars, you can adjust the scene and camera, as well as import your own art and even use 3D models. Sounds powerful, right? Also sounds like overkill. At the time of this writing, the basic "Quick" edition, while it has many templates, is a whopping $250 USD.

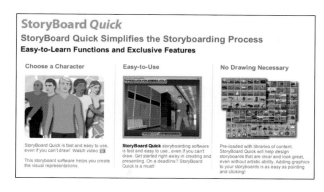

FIGURE 7.7
StoryBoard Artist.

Aside from the price tag, I have other reservations about using software like this for the comics you want to create. Tools like *StoryBoard Artist* are heavily focused on generated 3D environments.

One problem with using these 3D environments is that they tend to take away from the abstraction that makes comics so accessible. In fact, 3D models that try to mimic reality too much often run into a known problem called *Uncanny Valley*[4]—an uneasiness that people feel with animation that feels close to real but not real.

If you've ever seen films like *Final Fantasy: The Spirits Within*, *Polar Express* with Tom Hanks, or *Beowulf*, you'll already know what I'm talking about. The *Uncanny Valley* is a term coined by roboticist Masahiro Mori to describe how something (in his case, robots) that is too close to being human—but not quite—often creates a very overt negative reaction, while something that only vaguely resembles humans does not suffer from the same reactions.

If you really want a 3D scene generator, you might try looking in the realm of online games or communities. For example, Second Life[5] has pretty powerful customization tools and is an open environment that you can use to pose characters and scenes. In fact, there already are comics out there created using *Second Life* (see Figure 7.8)!

---

4 http://en.wikipedia.org/wiki/Uncanny_valley

5 http://secondlife.com

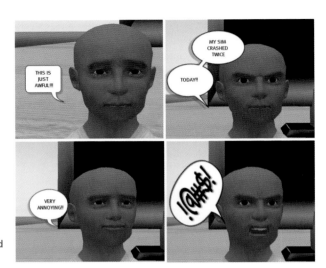

FIGURE 7.8
Comic snippet, created using *Second Life*.

There are even some tools available for use within the *Second Life* world to help making comics easier. One such tool is called *Murku* (see Figure 7.9) and is an interface you load while playing *Second Life*. In the creator's words:

"Murku is designed to facilitate the construction of comics based on content in a *Second Life* , i.e., SL environment. Murku will be of interest to those who have always dreamt of creating their own comics but who find the drawing of comics either too challenging or too laborious."

FIGURE 7.9
Murku: Second Life comic creation tool.

While tools like *Second Life* avoid the hefty price tag, you still have those eerie 3D models. With *StoryBoard Artist*, you'll find a "sketch mode," which allows you to convert the models to something that feels more like a sketch.

One last character and scene generator that's worth mentioning is *Poser*[6] from Smith Micro (see Figure 7.10). It's another desktop software and its beginner version is only $50. According to the site's information:

"Finally there's an easy way to learn 3D and be creative, even if you can't draw or have never taken an art class. Poser Debut is a 3D playground. Create scenes, add 3D characters, pose them, animate them, and make cool images or videos. It's easy. It's fun. It's Poser Debut."

FIGURE 7.10
Poser—your personal 3D playground.

Poser comes with a large collection of scenes and characters so it could be a great starting point. But your best bet is to use these generated scenes and characters as references and...you guessed it...trace them!

If these generators seem overwhelming to you, there's an even simpler solution. As comics have gained popularity, a few have taken it upon themselves to create common templates and generously shared them with the community.

---

6 http://poser.smithmicro.com/

Templates

One of these innovators was Martin Hardee. He wanted to create a few comics to communicate his product ideas and hired an illustrator. Instead of just creating the comics, he had the illustrator create a vast range of templates and scenarios common to describing computer and mobile use cases and then offered up the library of templates for others to contribute to.[7]

Similarly, Yvonne Shek and her colleagues at nForm, whose case study I share in Chapter 8, "Applying Comics," created a template to be reused in what they call their "Scenario Description Swimlanes" methodology. In their case, they hired a professional comic illustrator and created a template similar to the panels I presented in the previous chapter.

The use of templates such as this is definitely a potential shortcut to getting your comic created. Here's an example in Figure 7.11 of a few templates from Martin.

FIGURE 7.11
Sample of Design Comics template.

As you can see, there is a lot of variety: different camera angles, different characters, use of phones, and much more. You can see how creating a comic could be a cinch by just putting a few of these panels together and adding some dialogue. But like Yahoo! Avatars, you need to be careful not to limit your story based on the template. If you know what story you want to tell and these templates can effectively tell that story, then do it!

One other thing to watch out for with these templates is their photo-realistic quality. Although not as distracting as using actual photographs, they still lose some of the value of being abstract drawings. The realism of the faces

---

7 http://designcomics.org

also means the expressions are more nuanced rather than the exaggerated expressions you can do with more cartoon-like images. Here are two of the expressions in Martin's templates shown in Figure 7.12.

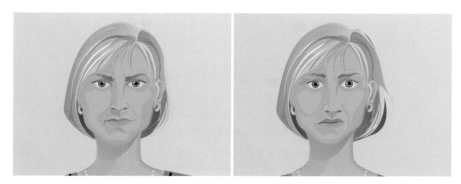

FIGURE 7.12
Two facial expressions in the Design Comics templates.

As you can see, it's difficult to distinguish between the two. Is one irritated, while the other is angry? Are they both equal amounts of unhappy? Does it matter? Perhaps it's simply easier to show an abstract face with an upside-down smile.

Another clever template that does use abstract facial expressions is one created by Bryce Johnson (see Figure 7.13).[8] Instead of using an illustrator, Bryce posed some toys in different configurations and took photographs of them. I love this idea as it marries the abstraction of comics with the ease of taking photographs.

FIGURE 7.13
Bryce Johnson's toy comic template.

---

8 http://www.flickr.com/photos/brycej/collections/72157605791728828/

Beyond these two templates, there are also the reference templates I mentioned from Wally Wood and the one I provided in Chapter 6, "Laying Out the Comic."

While all of these templates are potentially useful, ideally, it's best to create your own template for your purposes. That way, you can add to the template as the need arises, and the initial investment starts to pay for itself when you're able to create these stories without creating any art at all.

Comic Creation Software

Thus far, I've been talking about tools to help you create the art for the comics. What if you have the art, but you want some tools to help you through the final steps of actually creating a comic layout?

There are a few desktop software options that can help you with comic creation. I've already talked about Storyboard Artist and Poser as generator tools. The same people who make Poser also make something called Manga Studio.[9] Like Poser, they have different versions at different price points, including a beginner package. If you recall, *manga* is the Japanese word for comics and often refers to comics created in that style.

Manga Studio takes the art you create and allows you to quickly refine it, add colors, effects, and lay out a comic. It also has common tools for comic creation, such as adding dialogue or sound effects, as shown in Figure 7.14.

FIGURE 7.14
Manga Studio.

---

9 http://manga.smithmicro.com/

If even that seems like overkill for you, then the software you're looking for is Comic Life 2.[10] Comic Life 2 is an application for both Mac and Windows that lets you lay out images (whether they are photos or drawings) in any sort of comic layout you desire and quickly add captions, dialogue, and sound effects (see Figure 7.15).

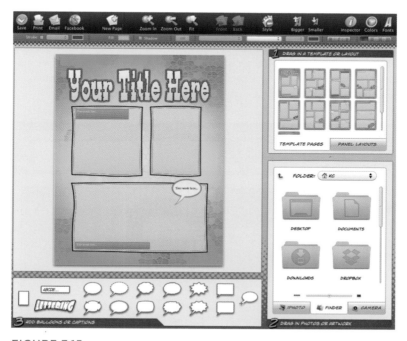

FIGURE 7.15
Comic Life 2.

The application includes a ton of fun fonts, various types of speech bubbles, and a lot of control over your comic's layout with one of the easiest interfaces. There is even an iPad version of the application.

The popular food blog, *The Amateur Gourmet,*[11] as a bit of a lark, wrote one of their reviews completely in comic form. The earlier example of a photo comic (refer to Figure 7.4) is from that blog. Much to the author's surprise (but not much to mine), the post was one of the most popular the author had ever written, and he's created many more comics since.

He used Comic Life to create it, and by his account, did so in a fairly short period of time. If you've already sketched the art, there's no better tool out there, especially for the price.

10 http://plasq.com/products/comiclife2

11 http://www.amateurgourmet.com/category/comics

Online Creation Tools

Aside from desktop software, there are also a few great online tools available now for creating comics from scratch. They're a hybrid of the tools I've mentioned, combining templates with layout tools. One website, BitStrips,[12] is a community site where people create comics using the tools available on the site and share these comics. Some of the comics created on the site have run for hundreds of episodes!

Like other tools mentioned in this chapter, BitStrips has a lot of built-in characters and scenes you can drop into a comic and resize or move (see Figure 7.16). You can also choose from a set of layouts and easily add captions and dialogue. It's quite the one-stop shop for comic creation.

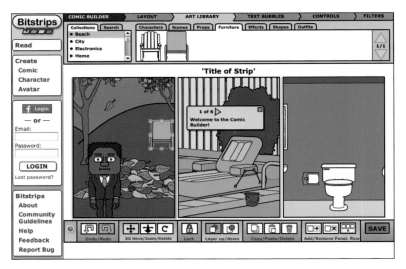

FIGURE 7.16
BitStrips templates.

What impressed me about the tool was that you could also create your own characters and scenes from their foundational pieces. For example, you could pick a set of eyes, a mouth, a nose, and body/face shapes and make a character of your own. You can then save this character and reuse it in your comics. For each character, there's a surprising amount of control over their expressions, appearances, body language, and even angle.

---

12 http://bitstrips.com

I'm personally not a fan of BitStrips' art style, but this is completely subjective. If the art style isn't a problem for you, this is definitely a resource you should consider using.

Another, newer, online comic creation tool is called Pixton (see Figure 7.17).[13] Like BitStrips, Pixton allows you to create comics on their website and then share them. They have characters you can choose from and a lot of scenes. I found their interface easier to use than BitStrips. In addition, their characters have more flexibility in how they can be posed, and the faces have more expressions.

FIGURE 7.17
Pixton.

I don't think any tool, even one as easy to use as *Pixton*, is faster than drawing your own stick figure sketches. But if you want to invest a little bit more time in a comic, I highly recommend trying this tool out. In fact, the *Pixton* creators have kindly created this comic for the book, showcasing the capabilities of their tool (see Figures 7.18 and 7.19).

---

13 http://pixton.com

A NEW WAY TO MAKE COMICS

Pixton gives you maximum expressive and creative control with flexible characters, freestyle panel layouts, and an award-winning interface.

Plus, with Team Comics™ you and your friends can work on the SAME COMIC at the SAME TIME!

Join the fun at Pixton.com – it's click-n-drag easy!

FIGURE 7.18
Pixton page 1.

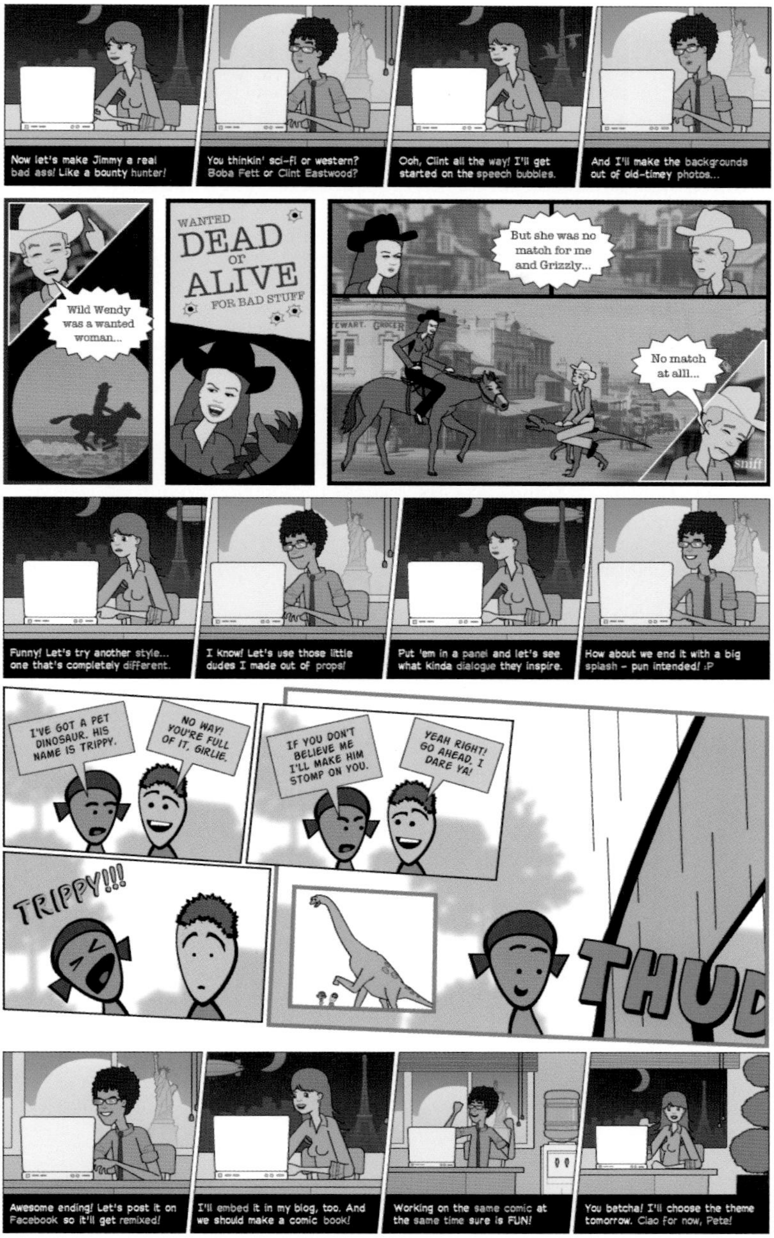
Now let's make Jimmy a real bad ass! Like a bounty hunter!
You thinkin' sci-fi or western? Boba Fett or Clint Eastwood?
Ooh, Clint all the way! I'll get started on the speech bubbles.
And I'll make the backgrounds out of old-timey photos...
Wild Wendy was a wanted woman...
WANTED DEAD or ALIVE FOR BAD STUFF
But she was no match for me and Grizzly...
No match at alll...
sniff
Funny! Let's try another style... one that's completely different.
I know! Let's use those little dudes I made out of props!
Put 'em in a panel and let's see what kinda dialogue they inspire.
How about we end it with a big splash – pun intended! :P
I'VE GOT A PET DINOSAUR. HIS NAME IS TRIPPY.
NO WAY! YOU'RE FULL OF IT, GIRLIE.
IF YOU DON'T BELIEVE ME I'LL MAKE HIM STOMP ON YOU.
YEAH RIGHT! GO AHEAD, I DARE YA!
TRIPPY!!!
THUD
Awesome ending! Let's post it on Facebook so it'll get remixed!
I'll embed it in my blog, too. And we should make a comic book!
Working on the same comic at the same time sure is FUN!
You betcha! I'll choose the theme tomorrow. Ciao for now, Pete!

FIGURE 7.19
Pixton page 2.

Summary

By now, you should be playing around with a slew of nifty comic creation tools and references. You might also have been side-tracked by reading a few comics along the way. (I know I was.) In this chapter, you learned how you can use some external resources to power up your comics.

- You can use images you find online as a way to reference what you need to draw.

- There are character and scene generators you can customize and then use as starting points for your comics.

- Some desktop software makes the process of laying out a comic and adding dialogue easier.

- Online comic creation tools are becoming more powerful and easier to use. Sometimes, they can be all you need to make your comics.

- Trace, trace, and trace!

Now that you have all the tools to make great comics, what do you do with them? As you'll see, there are a lot of different ways you can use them in your organization!

CHAPTER 8

Applying Comics

OK, NOW YOU'RE READY TO MAKE SOME COMICS! LET'S TALK ABOUT SOME MORE WAYS YOU CAN USE THEM.

THE USE THAT I'VE TALKED ABOUT MOST IS TO *COMMUNI-CATE VISION*.

COMICS ARE SUC-CINCT AND CONVEY FEATURES...

User has the ability to swipe credit card through reader connected to a smartphone (iphone or android).

Any major credit card is accepted.

...IN THE CONTEXT OF REAL USE CASES.

JUST SWIPE YOUR CARD ON THE PHONE.

WHICH IS A GREAT WAY TO START A PROJECT.

WHAT DO YOU THINK?

AS MOBILE APP *FOODSPOTTING* DID FOR 6 MONTHS BEFORE ANY CODING!

Satisfy your cravings
Whether you're a discriminating foodie or want to make the most of limited time or money, Foodspotting can help you find the best of any food in any city.

YOU CAN SHOW COMICS TO *POTEN-TIAL USERS* TO TEST YOUR ASSUMP-TIONS.

FIRST YOU ALLOW THE READER TO READ THE COMIC. ONCE ON THEIR OWN...

AND ONCE ALOUD, TO MAKE SURE THEY IN-TERPRETED THE STORY CORRECTLY.

AS THEY READ IT AGAIN, YOU CAN ASK FOR FEEDBACK. IN PARTICULAR...

HOW DOES THIS RELATE TO YOU?

WELL, I WOULDN'T USE THIS BUT MY FRIEND DAVE...

COMICS ARE ALSO GREAT FOR *MARKETING*. WHETHER THAT'S IN THE FORM OF A POSTCARD...

A WEBSITE HOMEPAGE...

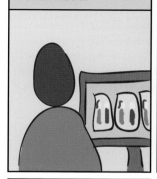

OR AN ADVERTISEMENT.

I'VE SEEN COMICS USED IN *JOURNALISM*...

IN *HISTORY* BOOKS...

AND EVEN IN *PROCESS DOCUMENTS*.

SO IT SEEMS, WE SHOULD AT LEAST CONSIDER USING COMICS IN ALMOST ANY SITUATION!

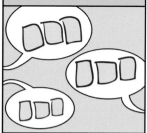

P resumably, when you started creating your comics, you already had some idea of how you wanted to use them. But you may be surprised to find how many different ways comics can be applied to your work. Although I follow the use of comics quite closely, I'm still surprised by how many new, creative applications are emerging.

I should preface this with a disclaimer: I'm not the type who believes in a method and then preaches its application for everything. Although there are many ways to use comics, it's not always the most appropriate solution to a problem. That said, there are a remarkable range of ways you can apply comics.

Communicating Vision

For the majority of this book, and in the Square example I've been using, I've been talking about creating a comic to show the idea for a product. These concept comics are a quick way to illustrate an idea to everyone: "Here's how people will use our product."

Typically, when you talk about what product you want to build, you communicate it through screenshots or requirements. After all, the word in a requirements document is "requirements," as in "what is required to build this product." Organizations are so accustomed to requirements documents that the need for them is rarely questioned. Imagine if you did stop to question the practice:

> Manager: "What are you doing?"
>
> You: "Writing a requirements document."
>
> Manager: "What for?"
>
> You: "So we can agree on what we're building, and so the engineers know exactly what to build."
>
> Manager: "How long is it?"
>
> You: "About 50 pages."
>
> Manager: "Who's going to read that?"
>
> You: "I was hoping you and the engineers."
>
> Manager: "I probably won't have the time or the patience. I'll pretend I did though and then later I'll ask why we're building it that way."
>
> You: "So...I shouldn't bother writing this document?"
>
> Manager: "Oh no, of course you should write a requirements document. How are we going to know what we're building otherwise?"
>
> You: "That's what I thought."

People don't question the need for requirements documents because it's really the only solution they know. How else can a project define what is required but with a document stating the requirements?

The sad fact is that most documentation doesn't get read. You may have heard of the term RTFM, which stands for "Read the F***ing Manual." The term was coined because so many consumers ask unnecessary questions that are already answered in the manual. But they don't read the manual because it's not easy to read. The same can be said for requirements documents.

What if, before a requirements document, or in addition to it, there was a comic or two explaining what the heck this product was supposed to do? The likelihood that everyone on the team would read a short comic about what a product should do is much higher than having them read a 50-page—or even a single-page—document.

Getting on the Same Page

Having everybody reading the requirements document before a project starts isn't just bureaucratic nonsense; it also ensures there are no surprises at the end. The problem is that requirements documents use words like "community," "leverage," "user-generated content," or other buzzwords *du jour* that seem meaningful but are rife with ambiguities.

Each person develops his or her own interpretation of what these words and phrases mean and thinks everyone else's interpretation is the same as his or her own. "These requirements look good," thinks the marketer. "Yep, looks about right to me," agrees the product manager. "Alright, I'll go build it according to this document then," says the engineer.

If instead, a comic illustrating the story of how someone may potentially use the product were shared among the team, it would be much easier to determine if everyone were on the same page.

For example, with Yahoo! Local, there was a lot of enthusiasm over the next version being all about "community," but the interpretation of that word differed from person to person. When comics were used to describe just how people would be using the new Yahoo! Local in the context of their lives, it was much easier to visualize the product and its features.

Comics aren't just used for getting on the same page about an upcoming product. You can also use comics to communicate processes or to draw parallels to a physical world.

Deb Aoki has many hats. She's a professional comic artist and the editor for the Manga section of about.com. She's also a senior content strategist and visual facilitation specialist at eBay and has contributed to eBay adopting the use of comics for more than just product concepts. On one of their products, eBay Shopping Cart, they used comics in a number of ways. Here's Deb on a couple of comics they used on the project:

"We did a lot of sketching/storyboarding for the Shopping Cart project. Some of it was to get buy-in from execs/partners. Some was to do problem solving during brainstorming sessions. We also used it for user research, too.

The first diagram (Figure 8.1), "cart flows," shows the buyer's journey from considering an item to checking out. The blue to green arrow in the middle is meant to show the change of the buyer's mood/intent as they go from "just browsing" to "I really want to buy this."

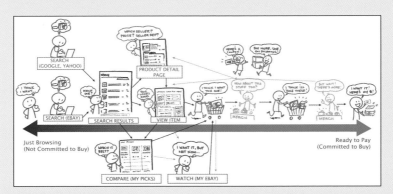

FIGURE 8.1
eBay cart flow.

The second diagram (Figure 8.2), "cart challenges," shows the problem with the shopping cart on eBay. Since many items listed are the one and only item available from a listing, the danger was that a buyer would put an item in their cart, then find later that someone else bought the item while it was in their cart. eBay doesn't reserve items while they're in the cart, so this was a real concern. I thought it would be humorous/relatable to use a grocery shopping/offline metaphor, rather than a purely eBay/online shopping scenario.

FIGURE 8.2
eBay cart challenges.

A Great Starting Point

Alexa Andrzejewski, the cofounder of the mobile start-up Foodspotting, created a one-pager that was comic-like, as the first step in her start-up (see Figure 8.3).

> "The very first thing I did, before I ever opened up Photoshop or put down a line of prototyping code, was to capture the core ideas behind Foodspotting in a one-page poster."

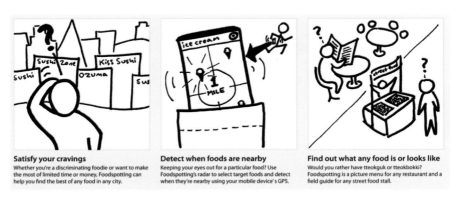

Satisfy your cravings
Whether you're a discriminating foodie or want to make the most of limited time or money, Foodspotting can help you find the best of any food in any city.

Detect when foods are nearby
Keeping your eyes out for a particular food? Use Foodspotting's radar to select target foods and detect when they're nearby using your mobile device's GPS.

Find out what any food is or looks like
Would you rather have tteokguk or tteokbokki? Foodspotting is a picture menu for any restaurant and a field guide for any street food stall.

FIGURE 8.3
Foodspotting comic.

This comic was not only used to set the tone for what the product would be and do, but it was also used in investor meetings to help them get funding. They didn't only use the one-pager for themselves, though. Alexa continues:

> "I used this poster to do some 'customer discovery.' I ate out a lot and shared my poster with anyone who would listen, which enabled me to validate and refine my ideas. Over the course of these six months, as I solidified my vision through paper prototypes and image map prototypes, what began as a literal 'Yelp for Dishes' evolved into the 'Visual guide to food and where to find it' that it is today, and by the time I found my cofounder Ted, who also happens to be the world's fastest, or at least most fearless, coder, we were able to hit the ground running and launch a beta within a month."

Which brings us to another application of comics: using them to validate your ideas with potential users.

Validating Ideas

Imagine getting these kinds of responses to your product before you even start building it:

> "I think my friend would really get a kick out of this."

> "I don't think that's very useful to me."

> "You've got to be in trouble with your girlfriend to go through all that hassle."

These are some of the responses we got on some proposed Yahoo! Local features we had, but we didn't get the responses by just describing the features. Nor did we spend time building prototypes of the features. We got these responses from showing comic scenarios to potential users.

Mark Wehner, the user researcher I worked with at Yahoo! Local, came up with the idea of showing these comics to potential users of the product. This idea was a huge success, and the feedback helped us refine some ideas and outright remove others.

Showing stories to participants provides them with a context they would otherwise be missing from just looking at screenshots. Instead of having participants "think-aloud" about what they think a button will do, you can engage them in an experience they can put themselves in.

To use comics in this manner, you can simply show them to people you meet, as Alexa did. However, you can also formalize the process a little more. At Yahoo!, we printed out our comics (you can print one panel per page to ensure that it's big enough) and ran our participants through a process.

Read It Twice

If you are testing a prototype, you might have some tasks for the participant to perform. But with comics, it's a little different since there's no interface. The first step is to ask the participants to read the comic on their own to ensure they have time to digest the story before providing feedback on it. This initial reading also allows the participants to immerse themselves in the story without interruption.

Once they've finished reading it, have the participants go through the story a second time, aloud, and describe the story in their own words. This reading ensures that they've interpreted the story correctly.

Sometimes, we've found that a story was poorly written and completely misconstrued. If we didn't have them describe the story in their own words, the feedback we'd receive could be completely irrelevant, and inaccurate feedback is even worse than no feedback at all!

Solicit Feedback

As the participants read the comics the second time around, you can start to solicit feedback from them. Find out what about the story and product is intriguing, appealing, confusing, or complicated to them.

As I've mentioned before, one of the strengths of comics is their abstract nature, which allows readers to relate themselves or someone they know to the story. As your participants are giving feedback on the comics, make sure that you ask them explicitly to talk about how this relates to them. Some quotes I've heard include the following:

> "This would have been useful when I was ..."

> "I normally wouldn't do this, but I know this couple that would love this."

Talking about these real-world scenarios helps refine the use cases you're trying to serve. By asking them their own stories, you are building up a set of *real* use cases that your product will be serving, and you can also adjust your comic to represent these use cases.

Feedback on Comic vs. Concept

Remember how we asked the participants to describe the story back to you? One of the reasons we did this was to gauge whether the comic itself was conveying what you thought it was.

A brilliant idea may not be received well if the story describing the idea is poorly done. It's important to differentiate whether feedback, especially negative feedback, is directed toward the comic or the concept. Is the negativity because your participants don't understand what you're trying to say or because what you said isn't appealing to them?

Once you can separate these two types of feedback, you can act accordingly. When we realized that the language our character "George" used was so contrived that it became a distraction, we modified his dialogue. We adjusted the way the story was told rather than the story itself and then proceeded to show the new comic to the ensuing participants.

The wonderful thing about these simple comics was that we were literally able to make these adjustments within under an hour so that we could try the iterated versions right away. Just as we discovered what areas were appealing in a product concept, the feedback on the comic could also help uncover the barriers that potential users would have with using the product.

Yvonne Shek is the VP at an Edmonton-based design and consulting agency, nForm User Experience. Instead of just showing comics, Yvonne layered the comics on top of something they already had: a series of steps that outlined the flow of the product. They call this method Scenario Description Swimlanes (or SDS), an example of which is in Figure 8.4.

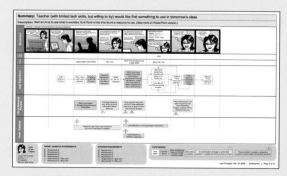

FIGURE 8.4
Scenario Description
Swimlanes.

How did you come up with this method?

We were developing workflows for the application. A lot of the people in the target audience are not in process engineering. The look of a flow chart scares them.

Before, we used the Scenario Description Swimlanes (SDS) without comics. We did a number of workshops with boxes and arrows to show the flow and this was fine when the audience was just the developers.

But with all kinds of people getting involved at different levels in the organization and different technical levels, we wanted a common language we could use. So we thought, "Why not add a layer?"

So on top of the flow, we included a comic version, using templates drawn by an illustrator we hired (although we did the initial sketches), which tells the story of the user going through those same steps. We could have written prose instead, but we felt this was the best way to get them to read it.

What were your audience's thoughts on the method?

They really liked it! Originally, they were a little surprised, but they thought it was cool. The SDS really cut down on the review time and buy-in. It even cut down on the design time. My colleague, Dennis, who designed the product at that time, had just started with nForm, and he had to do the user interface for the project. He just sat down and stared at the SDS for a week and then wireframes just came out and they were spot-on. The SDS acted like his requirements doc, and gave him context even though he had no background on the project up till that point in time.

Later, we ended up working with the same client, and they asked for the SDS again. I think that's a good sign.

Market Your Product

How did the United States Postal Service (USPS) utilize comics? One day, I received a comic in the mail from my dear friends at the post office. It was a comic strip from the popular Sunday comics, *Cathy*. If you're not familiar with the strip, it centers on a neurotic, frantic, yet endearing woman and her everyday trials.

In this particular strip, Cathy's boyfriend asked her if she had a stamp. She frantically looked through her purse, emptying a mountain of contents. Her boyfriend said it really wasn't necessary, because he could buy the stamp online, or at the grocery store, or even at an ATM. "It's in here somewhere," she exclaimed but too late, since he was already headed out the door.

My apartment complex had a wall of mailboxes and a very handy trough underneath to throw out any junk mail we received. Had this been a regular postcard from the post office, with bullet points explaining, "Did you know? You can now buy stamps at…." I would likely have dropped it into the bin without a second glance.

Instead, I took 15 seconds to read the comic before moving on. The *Cathy* comic was light-hearted and slightly humorous, but it also served as a stealthy vehicle to market the information to me.

If you think it's unlikely that your teammates read your documentation, imagine how hard it is to get potential customers to read your marketing copy explaining what your product does. Consumers are numb from the deluge of information, banner ads, and marketing speak they receive daily. They also have a plethora of data and information to distract them wherever they happen to be.

Even on a bus, traditionally the place where you're guaranteed to get the eyeballs of a captive audience, riders are now spending their commuting time on their phones or other Internet devices. In such an environment, the only way to get a person's attention and get your message across is to be brief and entertaining.

Unsurprisingly, comics excel both in being brief and entertaining! Best of all, if your organization used comics to define the product at the outset, you will have a template for your marketing material already.

At Raptr, the start-up where I used to work, we were trying to convey why our product was useful. We decided, rather than dwell on features, we'd explain the flow of how someone would use it. Figure 8.5 shows the comic we used.

FIGURE 8.5
Raptr comic.

Whether it's a narrative story or a step-by-step comic, the use of comics to introduce a product is becoming more and more common. The comics don't have to be short, either. As we discussed before, Google also used a long-form comic to explain why they created their Google Chrome browser. Its novelty and ease of reading gained a lot of attention.

An Alternative Medium

Comics are like a Trojan horse for information. The format of comics creates a natural gravitation toward them. They have a low barrier, are quick to read, and perhaps most importantly, are entertaining. Providing useful information in a comic is almost unfair to the reader because the humor and light-hearted nature lowers the reader's defenses.

So it's fair to say that comics should be considered for communicating any message. At times, a video, document, or prototype may be more appropriate, but you should always at least consider the medium. People have used comics to explain all sorts of topics.

In journalism, Dan Archer has collected a list of comic journalists—people who are journalists but document the story in comic form. Sometimes the comics are interactive, sometimes they are short, and other times they are entire novels.

Similarly, historic events have been documented in comic form. You may have heard of Howard Zinn's *People's History of the United States*. What you may not know is that there is a full graphic novel version of the story as well.

Some comics are historical but also autobiographical. One of the most acclaimed comics is Art Spiegelman's *Maus*, which documents his grandfather's experiences surviving the German concentration camps in World War II. Kaylin Andres and Jon Sol's *Terminally Illin'* and Marisa Acocella Marchetto's *Cancer Vixen: A True Story* both tell their respective personal battles with cancer. Who said comics were for kids?

Comics can also be used for educational purposes. There's an entire series of comics, called *Mange Guide to...*, which covers a range of subjects from physics and electricity to statistics and relativity. As we'll discuss in the next chapter, there's also scientific proof that this form may in fact be better for teaching.

I mentioned *Commitment*, the comic by Chris Matts, Olav Maassen, and Chris Geary on risk management, in Chapter 6, "Laying Out the Comic." Their comic (shown in Figure 8.6) is a great example demonstrating the intersection of education and business.

FIGURE 8.6
Commitment comic.

Not all of their comics are this level of production, either. Chris Matts, in particular, has been using low-fidelity comics for years, much like the ones we've been working with throughout this book, to convey how the Agile process works in organizations.

Speaking of business applications of comics, a few high-profile business books have either been translated to graphic novel form or started that way. Tony Hsieh, founder of the popular ecommerce site Zappos, wrote a book called *Delivering Happiness* and recently released a comic version. Daniel

What gave you the idea to write a business book in comic form? Why do a comic book?

It was a few things. First, back in 2007, I spent a couple of months in Japan studying the Manga industry. One of the things you quickly discover is that comics in Japan and comics in America have very different places in people's lives. In Japan, comics are ubiquitous. You can find manga for just about every topic—from time management to politics to history to investing. Meanwhile, manga was becoming extremely popular here in America. But it was still mostly for kids—and mostly about romance and supernatural adventures. That seemed way too limited. So I thought: Why not use this incredibly powerful expressive form to reinvent the business book?

Second, I began to think about the role of books in general in a world where people have so many other avenues to information. For career information in particular, it seemed that all the tactical information was available for free online. Putting that sort of info into a printed book didn't make much sense. But I did think there was value to readers in creating books that offered the sort of insights that couldn't be Googled—strategic, big picture advice. That's what I tried to do with the six big lessons in *The Adventures of Johnny Bunko*.

What do you think the biggest benefits were of doing a book in comic form?

Speed and "shareability." People can read the book in less than an hour. And because it's a paperback in a small format, they don't consider it some sort of priceless artifact that has to sit on their shelves. Instead, they pass the book to a friend and that friend gives it to someone else. This format is about as viral as a set of atoms can be.

What do you think are appropriate cases to use comics as the medium?

Just about any topic can work—provided there's a compelling story. That's the key. This format is more than simply pictures adorning words. The images exist to advance and deepen the narrative. A good story can overcome so-so art. But beautiful pictures can make up for a mediocre story.

Pink, a bestselling author of numerous books including *Drive* and *A Whole New Mind*, also wrote a book entirely in comic form. I had a chance to ask him a few questions about his book.

You may think all of these examples seem rather high production in value, but there are many instances of comics in use in organizations for more than just products. I've already talked a bit about how eBay uses comics. Aside from conveying product ideas, they also have used comics to convey process changes internally.

Similarly, Evangeline Haughney, a senior user researcher at Adobe, used comics to convey her research findings. She did this because she found that more people actually spent time reading her findings.

Whether it's to communicate news, marketing, processes, education, business, life, or a product, it seems that comics make a remarkable medium. Whenever you're looking to get a point across and want to make sure it gets read, you should consider, "Should I use a comic to communicate this?"

Summary

We've discussed how to create comics quickly without any need for an illustrator. In this chapter, I talked about different ways you can use comics throughout your process and how prevalent comics are in every industry and application. Comics can be used to:

- Communicate the vision of what you want to build.

- Validate your ideas.

- Market your product.

- Replace documentation of almost any form.

If you've gotten this far, I imagine you're convinced that comics are the way to go, and you want to get started using comics everywhere. The final question then, is how you convince everyone else to invest the time and resources to let you draw your stick figures? How do you make sure that they take you seriously? That's what we'll discuss in the last chapter.

CHAPTER 9

Breaking Down the Barriers

EVERY MEDIUM RUNS INTO SOME RESISTANCE AT FIRST.

WHO WANTS TO HEAR THEIR VOICE? HA! SILLY TALKIES.

COMICS ARE STARTING TO MATURE BEYOND "NOVELTY" STATUS.

TIME MAGAZINE BEST BOOK OF 2006

FUN HOME

BUT WE'RE NOT QUITE THERE YET. SO YOU MIGHT HAVE SOME CONVINCING TO DO.

YOU WANT TO USE *WHAT*?

THE FIRST STEP IS TO FIGURE OUT WHO YOU'RE CONVINCING.

AND MORE IMPORTANTLY, WHAT THEIR CONCERNS WILL BE.

AS WE'VE DISCUSSED AND SEEN AT YAHOO!, COMICS CAN SAVE YOU *TIME* BY GETTING ON THE SAME PAGE EARLY.

AND IT MAKES THE TIME TO REVIEW DOCUMENTS FASTER, TOO.

I WENT THROUGH THAT REALLY QUICKLY!

COMICS ARE ACTUALLY GREAT VALUE WHEN IT COMES TO UPFRONT INVESTMENT.

SKILLS AND RESOURCES NEEDED

SCRIPTS
DRAWINGS
COMICS
PERSONAS
USE CASES
WIREFRAMES
VIDEO
ANIMATION
INTERACTIVE PROTOTYPE

SOME   A LOT

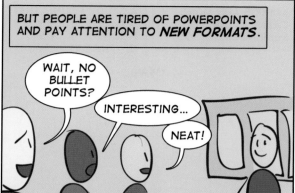

YOU MIGHT THINK PEOPLE WILL LAUGH YOU OUT OF THE ROOM IF YOU SHOW THEM A COMIC.

COMICS?! HA!

BUT PEOPLE ARE TIRED OF POWERPOINTS AND PAY ATTENTION TO *NEW FORMATS*.

WAIT, NO BULLET POINTS?

INTERESTING...

NEAT!

HOW COMICS ARE RECEIVED DEPENDS ON YOUR PRESENTATION OF THEM.

HOW YOU *FRAME* YOUR PRESENTATION IS IMPORTANT.

REMEMBER THAT COMICS ARE JUST A VEHICLE FOR YOUR IDEA, AND THE IDEA IS WHAT'S IMPORTANT.

INSTEAD OF...

DO YOU UH...WANT TO SEE THIS...COMIC I MADE?

...MAYBE?

TRY...

I'D LIKE TO REVIEW THIS STORYBOARD FOR OUR PRODUCT CONCEPT.

BELIEVE IN THE MEDIUM AND CONCEPT AND EVERYONE ELSE WILL, TOO!

COMICS ARE MORE LIKELY TO BE REMEMBERED, TOO.

A STUDY FOUND THAT COLLEGE STUDENTS WHO READ A COMIC ON THE PROCESS OF LIGHTNING RECALLED BETTER.

AT RAPTR, WHEN WE COMPARED TWO HOMEPAGE DESIGNS...

THE ONE WITH A COMIC HAD TWICE AS MANY SIGNUPS!

SO YOU EVEN HAVE THE BACKING OF *SCIENCE*!

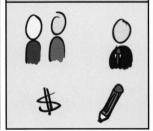

SOMETIMES, ORGANI-ZATIONS JUST NEED TO SEE EXAMPLES FROM OTHER RESPECTABLE COMPANIES.

AND YOU HAVE PLENTY OF EXAMPLES!

THE BIGGEST BARRIER TO USING COMICS MAY NOT BE YOUR PEERS, MANAGERS, TALENT, OR BUDGET.

BUT INSTEAD, IT MAY BE YOUR OWN APPREHENSION!

Up until about five years ago, the medium of comics (or graphic novels) was largely regarded as children's entertainment. Although there were artistic works being created beyond the standard Sunday strips and *Superman* fare, little recognition was given. Today, graphic novels such as *Persepolis* find themselves on the *New York Times Bestsellers* list and others such as *V for Vendetta* and *Sin City* are adapted to feature length films.

In many ways, comics have been going through a similar rite of passage as photography, music, television, and film. Each ran into problems with acceptance within the mainstream. Photography was believed to steal the soul from its subjects, jazz music was considered to be the devil's music, and film went through numerous stages of belittlement and ridicule before being taken seriously.

All this is to say that comics have matured beyond being a novelty. Their mainstream legitimacy becomes more apparent every year. Obviously, this matters to you if you want to use comics to communicate your ideas.

If you were to show a video that showcased your vision for your product's experience, it would generally be a pretty accepted practice (assuming you had the time, money, and expertise to take on such an endeavor). If you were to propose that the company use a jingle for an advertisement, that, too, would be considered quite normal.

For now, proposing to use comics for any purpose can run into internal and external obstacles. Until comics truly do become aligned with other media, you might need to overcome a few barriers.

Understand Your Audience

Just as there are different ways to use comics and different audiences to create comics for, the type of resistance you'll encounter may differ depending on to whom you're presenting.

Most commonly, people find they run into difficulties trying to get buy-in from management or a client in order to get the budget, time, and people to create a comic.

Another common fear is how executives or stakeholders you're reporting to (such as clients) would receive proposals sent their way as comics.

Perhaps you're worried about how well your comics will be received by your peers, and whether the work will be taken seriously if it is in comic form.

Similar worries may exist as to what customers' reactions would be like if you were to use comics as a form of marketing.

Once you understand which of these buckets you fall under, it becomes much easier to overcome the inherent barriers because you can then address specific concerns relevant to your audience.

Sell the Time Savings

I'm often told, "I'd love to do this at my organization, but I think I would have trouble convincing my colleagues and my manager to give me the time to do so."

Notice the "I think" part of that statement. I can't recall a time when anyone has told me that they specifically asked to employ comics in their work and had been rejected. In nearly every company I've interviewed, ranging from Google and eBay to smaller consultancies, the acceptance of the medium as a tool involved much less friction than you might imagine.

Having said that, there are certainly strategies to keep you prepared. Preston Smalley, Director of User Experience at eBay, was one of the champions of employing comics to communicate ideas there. He relayed his experiences for convincing others to buy in:

> "Fundamentally, it required the belief that if you think through the experience of the user up front, then it saves you time beyond."

"Saves you time" is a key phrase there that should perk up the ears of anyone in the corporate world. Ultimately, we already spend a great deal of time on documentation. We create marketing requirement documents, technical requirement documents, use cases, market segmentations, user profiles and personas, and many more artifacts before even starting to build.

Imagine if just a bit of that time were spent on a single document explaining how the user would experience your product: a document that could unify the vision and be used as a guidepost for the development process. You could be saving your organization a lot of backtracking and confusion later on.

When you compare comics against other tools available, it doesn't even require that much time in comparison. Figure 9.1 shows a modified chart of one created by Gayle Curtis and Laurie Vertelney that illustrates how much effort and skill is required by some of these tools. The chart is a bit dated, as skills such as prototyping have become significantly easier, but as you can see, creating comics is one of the cheapest options. (If you're interested in prototyping, you should definitely check out Todd Zaki Warfel's book: *Prototyping: A Practitioner's Guide*.)

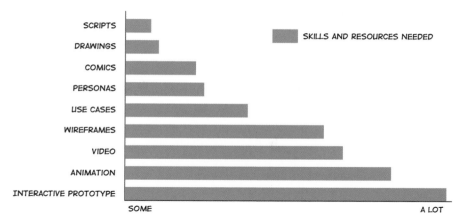

FIGURE 9.1
Resources and skill required for various techniques.

Another example of concrete time-savings is the Yahoo! Local project I discussed in Chapter 1, "Comics?!" With that project, instead of discovering three months into the development cycle that there was a major disconnect between different people's viewpoints, we could have ensured we were all on the same page right from the beginning. Comparatively, the process of creating the comics would have taken one week and would have been read by the whole team, ensuring that everyone was in agreement on the direction. In comparison to three months of wasted development time, the investment for comics would have been trivial.

Beyond the time savings, Preston also took care in how he presented the opportunity:

> "We sold them on the idea that you need to have the concept of what you want to do. We didn't sell the drawing."

In other words, Preston didn't focus on the medium at all. Instead, he focused on the need for a story and a vision and allowed comics to be just the vehicle he happened to use to convey that vision.

Can you convince your organization that you need a few days or a week to brainstorm and document the vision of what the product should do? That sounds a lot more palatable than convincing your organization that you need a week to create a comic.

It's All About Framing

Supposing that you've already created a comic. Now you're wondering about how best to present this to an executive or a potential client without being laughed out of the room. "They'll think I'm trying to bring them back to kindergarten," you might be thinking.

That may very well happen if you present them with kindergarten drawings. Remember that the fidelity and quality of your comic should scale with the audience. Stick figures are fine for your colleagues, but generally may not be as effective for executive presentations. This isn't specific to comics, though. Anything you present to stakeholders is likely to have more polish than internal documents.

Design consultancies such as nForm and Adaptive Path have been using comics with potential and active clients with great success. Yvonne Shek, who was working on the Scenario Description Swimlanes method we featured in Chapter 8, "Applying Comics," said this of the client:

> "Originally, they were a little surprised, but they thought it was cool. 'Y'know what? I went through that really quickly,' they said. It really cut down on review time and buy-in. It also cut down on design time."

Preston from eBay also found that using them in presentations wasn't all that challenging:

> "eBay is a very presentation- and PowerPoint-centric culture. This was a different form of presentation so it was easier."

What organization these days *isn't* presentation- and PowerPoint-centric? Using comics may actually be a refreshing change from the dull presentation formats that most people are used to. After all, presentations are largely about packaging—something that comics are well suited to.

One of the most talented packagers was former Apple CEO Steve Jobs. When he presented his annual MacWorld keynotes, the audience was enthralled. His slides, created by Duarte Design (who also created the visuals for Al Gore's *An Inconvenient Truth*), were often given much of the credit.

The content was not all that different from a standard PowerPoint. There were graphs, pie charts, some tables, and some screenshots. Yet something about the way it was packaged and presented made the presentation unique.

Jobs had more than just visual flair in his presentations, though. Another aspect of his (and Apple's) presentations was the choice of words he used. If you pay attention to them, you'll notice a rather gratuitous use of words such as "awesome," "incredible," and "amazing"—so much so that you can now find YouTube videos that have condensed an Apple presentation to just their use of superlatives.

As amusing as that is, their enthusiasm is absolutely contagious. Every Apple presenter is genuinely enthused and believes in their products' greatness, but more importantly, they make absolutely sure you know it, too.

Even the names they use for their products and features are noteworthy. Instead of a high-resolution iPad or an iPhone with high definition (HD), they call the screens "Retina Display" because they're at a resolution where the human eye cannot distinguish individual pixels. Apple was not the first to have such high resolutions, but they branded them in a way that was easy for others to understand.

Similarly, your choice of words matters when you present your comics. Instead of, "check out this comic for our product idea," it could be, "I'd like to review this storyboard that describes our product concept." It's all in how you frame the work. Don't be ashamed of it or feel sheepish. If your confidence is behind it, it will show.

Believe in what a great medium it is and believe in your product concept. Then make absolutely sure that everyone also knows how awesome, incredible, and amazing they are.

It Gets Attention

In her study *Using Comics to Communicate Qualitative Research Findings,* Evangeline Haughney interviewed 18 participants and then created comics to describe each interviewee's habits and behavior.

These comics were presented to her peers at Adobe as a way to increase engagement and solve the problem of people not reading reports or being disengaged during a slide presentation.

Although the comics were made for her colleagues, Haughney was still wary of how they would be received. To help set expectations, she did some up-front legwork:

> Since a comic is not a traditional report, a lot of time must be spent campaigning to your audience prior to the deliverable. Paving the way with email teasers, including instructions within the comic, and then reinforcing the message during the hand-delivery can be time-consuming but necessary.

These steps can certainly help build anticipation and excitement. However, if you don't have the time to do such preparation, fret not.

Assuming your workplace is anything like the ones I've been in, I think a comic is much more likely to elicit a sigh of relief ("at least it's not another requirements document") than one of confusion.

Comics aren't just more likely to be read, but they're more likely to be remembered, too. In a research study published in the *Journal of Educational Psychology*, researchers presented some students with summaries of texts in comic form:

> In a series of three experiments, college students who read a summary that contained a sequence of short captions with simple illustrations depicting the main steps in the process of lightning recalled these steps and solved transfer problems as well as or better than students who received the full text along with the summary or the full text alone.

What the researchers found was the difference in medium improved recall *and* application. There's science behind the power of comics!

Everybody's Doing It

The truth is, comics are all around us. Companies everywhere are already using them for posters, manuals, homepages, information booklets, and more.

It's one thing to use comics for internal communication but deciding to use comics for customer-facing material is definitely a different level of commitment. Your organization is likely to be quite a bit more reticent to use comics in this manner. It may seem too risky or niche. It may alienate customers who aren't fans of comics. If that sounds like your organization, then you don't work at IKEA, LEGO, Google, Ford, or the U.S. Navy.

I mentioned Raptr last chapter and showed how we used a comic to market the product. We had agonized for hours over how best to convey all the cool things people could do on our social network. We played with carousels, core values propositions, and other buzzwords, but what ultimately helped us decide on the approach was the five-second litmus test.

We assumed that nobody would spend more than five seconds on our homepage if they couldn't figure out what we were and why they should care within that period.

This test forced us to focus on what the truly important message was. What would you try to tell a customer if you only had five seconds? It also constrained us from using bullet points or carousels to try and show people the kitchen sink on their first visit.

With these factors in mind, a comic was the best way to convey a use case ("this is how we're useful to you") in a story format that could be consumed in five seconds.

Ann Wylie is the words behind Communicating with Comics, a communication firm that helps organizations tell their stories and sell their messages through comics, graphic novels, and other forms of graphic storytelling (www.communicatingwithcomics.com). Ann is an International Association of Business Communicators (IABC) Gold Quill Award-winning writing expert. Her brother and partner, Bill Wylie, is a former Marvel Comics artist with more than 15 years of experience bringing organizations, brands, and people to life with visual storytelling.

If you need help creating comics, or proving that comics work, Ann is a great person to go to.

"Comics are for re-reading, not reading. They're harder not to read."

—Art Spiegelman, American comics artist best known for his Pulitzer Prize-winning graphic biography, *Maus*

When Campus Progress ran "An Education in For-Profit Education".[1] Susie Cagle's graphic story about education finance, the piece:

- Was featured on the front page of *The Huffington Post*.

- Was picked up by Lifehacker.

- Got more than 4,000 Facebook shares and likes.

- Garnered more than 700 Tweets.

- Received more than 800 comments.

Comics are a great way to get the word out about your topic. Organizations can also use graphic storytelling to do the following:

- Boost readership. Adding cartoons illustrating wound care instructions to the text increased readership by 24%, according to a 1996 study at the University of Michigan.

- Increase understanding. Students scored almost twice as high at knowing the differences between confusing word pairs (accept vs. except, for instance) if they looked at cartoons illustrating the examples instead of written examples only, researchers learned in a 2004 study at a large Midwestern university.

- Move people to act. Parents answered 25% more questions correctly when they watched an animated cartoon explaining the need for polio vaccines than when they read a leaflet covering the same material, according to a 2004 study at Texas Tech University.

---

1 http://bit.ly/hKC0tN

What's important to note about how Raptr arrived at using comics was the process. We didn't decide on the medium and then decide on the message. Once we understood the constraints we were working under, there was no convincing necessary: comics were clearly the way to go.

To add even more credibility, though, we also tested the comic homepage against a more traditional one that used bullet points to showcase the features. It was still a visual homepage, but it didn't convey a story about the product. We simultaneously ran both homepages, showing half the audience one and half the other.

What we found was that the comic homepage garnered *twice* as many sign-ups as the bullet-point version. Not only were the comics time saving, but they were also money generating!

IKEA and LEGO use comics for their construction manuals because they require manuals that are easy to translate and can be followed by anybody very easily. Google used comics to help promote Google Chrome's launch because they needed a form factor that was not as dense as a white paper, preserved the voices of the engineers, and conveyed a message beyond the "browser wars."

Sometimes, organizations just need to see examples from other, respectable companies. Once you showcase their use of comics and reinforce that with the time and money savings, it's difficult to argue against seriously considering comics for every stage of the product life cycle.

Summary

It can be daunting to propose using comics within your organization; however, there's mounting evidence that comics are a valuable tool.

- They are being used by many organizations, including Google, eBay, Adobe, IKEA, Ford, and more.

- They've been shown to increase comprehension.

- They save an organization time over the long term, thus saving money.

However, the biggest barrier to using comics may not be your peers, your managers, your budget, or your talent, but rather your own inhibitions. If you treat comics just like any other document and focus on the content of the message rather than the form, you're unlikely to find anyone who will challenge their use. Like photography, music, television, and film, it's all about acceptance.

CHAPTER 10

Wrapping Up

OH HI! I WASN'T EXPECTING YOU TO BE HERE SO SOON.

RAISE YOUR HAND IF YOU'RE HERE BECAUSE YOU READ THROUGH THE WHOLE BOOK.

HMMM. NOT MANY OF YOU.

WELL IF YOU DID SKIP AHEAD, I DON'T BLAME YOU.

COMICS HAVE THIS MAGNETIC DRAW. I CAN'T HELP BUT READ THEM OVER A BUNCH OF WORDS.

WHEN I STARTED THIS BOOK A FEW YEARS AGO...

ARE YOU DONE YET?

HOW'S THE BOOK GOING?

WE WERE STILL MOSTLY TIED TO COMPUTERS.

AND MOST OF THE PRODUCTS WE WERE DESIGNING WERE DESKTOP-BASED.

WHICH CAN LEAD TO SOME UNINTEREST-ING STORIES.

AND BACK THEN, COMICS WERE LESS ACCEPTED.

WHO WOULD WATCH AN *AVENGERS* MOVIE?!

BUT NOW, COMICS HAVE STARTED BECOMING MORE MAINSTREAM.

I'M MORE INTO THE MICHAEL KEATON ERA OF BATMAN MOVIES*.

*NOBODY REALLY THINKS THIS

COMPANIES LIKE *PIXAR* HAVE HELPED PEOPLE APPRECIATE THE ART OF STORY-TELLING.

COMPANIES LIKE *GOOGLE* HAVE HELPED PUSH THE IDEA OF COMICS IN BUSINESS.

IN THAT SAME PERIOD, THE WORLD BECAME MORE MOBILE.

PEOPLE ARE ON THEIR PHONES MUCH MORE...

NOT JUST ON PHONES; THERE ARE OTHER MOBILE DEVICES NOW, TOO.

DEVICES LIKE *FITBIT* AND *NIKE FUEL-BAND* TRACK YOUR MOVEMENT.

I JUST LEVELED UP TO GRAND-MASTER WALKER!

THERE ARE DEVICES THAT TRACK YOUR WEIGHT OVER TIME.

YOU SHOULD LAY OFF THOSE FRIES.

HEY!

AND EVEN YOUR SLEEP!

I HAVE TROUBLE SLEEPING SO I'M GOING TO WEAR THIS HEADBAND ALL NIGHT!

AS WE CREATE PRODUCTS FOR THESE DEVICES, *CONTEXT* BECOMES EVEN MORE IMPORTANT.

IS IT NOISY WHERE THEY ARE?

DO THEY HAVE AN INTERNET CONNECTION?

WILL THERE BE GLARE?

AND TELLING THE STORY OF HOW YOUR PRODUCT WILL BE USED MATTERS EVEN MORE.

ONE OTHER DEVELOPMENT IS THAT IT'S BECOME MUCH EASIER TO JUST BUILD SOMETHING.

LOOK MOM! I BUILT AN APP!

AND IT'S TEMPTING TO JUST BUILD THINGS RIGHT AWAY TO TRY THEM.

TRY THIS!

AND THIS!

NOW TRY THIS!

WAIT, TRY THIS!

BUT EVEN PROTOTYPES CAN'T ANSWER SOME QUESTIONS.

COMICS CAN BE USED TO HELP FIGURE OUT WHAT TO BUILD.

YOU CAN DRAW COMICS TO TELL WHAT THE STORY IS **NOW**.

WHAT SONG IS THAT?

I DUNNO...

ADELE?

NO...

LATER...

DANG, I WISH I KNEW WHAT THAT SONG WAS...

LYRICS SEARCH

WHICH WILL HELP YOU IDENTIFY WHAT PROBLEMS NEED FIXING.

THIS SUCKS!

AND THEN YOU CAN DRAW COMICS ABOUT HOW YOUR PRODUCT CHANGES THE STORY.

WHAT SONG IS THAT?

WHAT'RE YOU DOING?

YEP. IT'S ADELE.

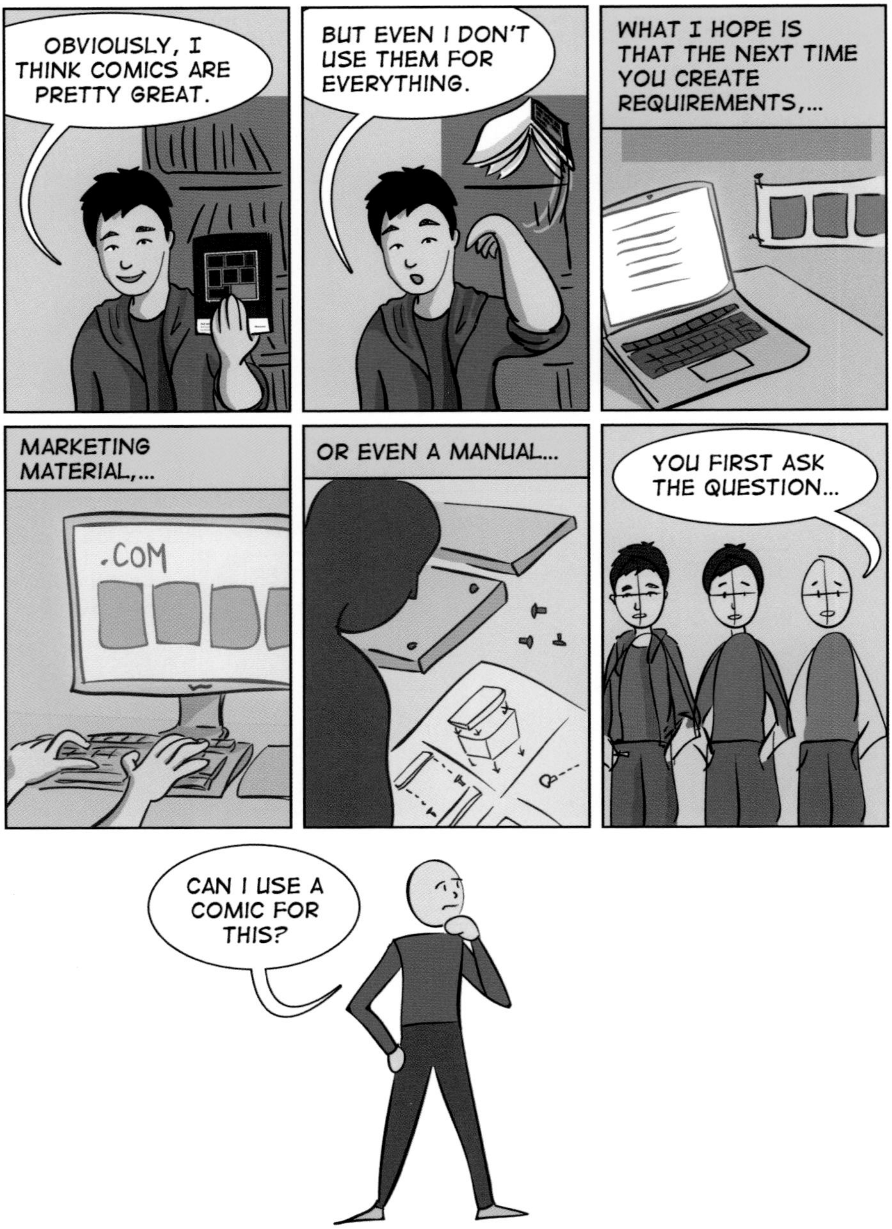
OBVIOUSLY, I THINK COMICS ARE PRETTY GREAT.
BUT EVEN I DON'T USE THEM FOR EVERYTHING.
WHAT I HOPE IS THAT THE NEXT TIME YOU CREATE REQUIREMENTS,...
MARKETING MATERIAL,...
.COM
OR EVEN A MANUAL...
YOU FIRST ASK THE QUESTION...
CAN I USE A COMIC FOR THIS?

Useful Templates and References

ere are a few handy pages to use as reference when you're creating your comics. Feel free to use these as templates or just to refer to when creating your comics.

FIGURE A.1
Different ways to show someone on the computer.

Interesting Comic Panels

A lot of times, you're drawing someone using a computer (Figure A.1) or a mobile device (Figure A.2) from panel to panel. In order to keep it interesting, refer to these templates for variations on the same theme. When you pick the angle, think about how much of the interface you wish to show.

FIGURE A.2
Different ways to show someone on a phone.

Gesture Dictionary

Body language can convey much about a person's emotions and state of mind (Figure A.3). A hunch here, a crossed arm there, and you have completely different meanings. Even when you draw a stickman with no face, you can show emotion. These examples are inspired by Will Eisner's *Comics and Sequential Art*.

ANGER

FEAR

JOY

FRUSTRATION

PENSIVE

PUZZLED

FIGURE A.3
Body language for various emotions.

Facial Expression Dictionary

Remember that facial expressions are primarily conveyed through the eyebrows and the mouth. These three simple lines can communicate everything. Experiment with different shapes and don't be afraid to exaggerate (see Figure A.4). Subtlety is not really what comics are about.

UNSATISFIED   FRUSTRATED   ANGRY   SURPRISED (BAD)

SATISFIED   HAPPY   OVERJOYED   SURPRISED (GOOD)

PENSIVE   CONCENTRATION   PUZZLED   BAFFLED

DOUBTFUL   STRESSED   EXCITED   INDIFFERENT

FIGURE A.4
Facial expression dictionary.